Walking with
Gospel Women

Text copyright © Fiona Stratta 2012
The author asserts the moral right
to be identified as the author of this work

Published by
The Bible Reading Fellowship
15 The Chambers, Vineyard
Abingdon OX14 3FE
United Kingdom
Tel: +44 (0)1865 319700
Email: enquiries@brf.org.uk
Website: www.brf.org.uk
BRF is a Registered Charity

ISBN 978 0 85746 010 3

First published 2012
10 9 8 7 6 5 4 3 2 1 0
All rights reserved

Acknowledgments
Unless otherwise stated, Bible quotations are taken from the Holy Bible, New Living
Translation, copyright © 1996, 2004. Used by permission of Tyndale House Publishers, Inc.,
Wheaton, Illinois 60189. All rights reserved.

Scripture quotations taken from the Holy Bible, New International Version®, NIV® Copyright
© 1973, 1978, 1984, 2011 by Biblica, Inc.™ Used by permission. All rights reserved
worldwide.

Scripture taken from the Holy Bible, New International Version®. Copyright © 1973, 1978,
1984 Biblica. Used by permission of Hodder & Stoughton Publishers, a member of the
Hachette Livre UK Group. All rights reserved.

The Living Bible copyright © 1971 by Tyndale House Publishers.

Scripture quotations from THE MESSAGE. Copyright © by Eugene H. Peterson 1993, 1994,
1995. Used by permission of NavPress Publishing Group.

Scripture quotations from The New Revised Standard Version of the Bible, Anglicised Edition,
copyright © 1989, 1995 by the Division of Christian Education of the National Council of the
Churches of Christ in the United States of America, are used by permission. All rights reserved.

The paper used in the production of this publication was supplied by mills that source their
raw materials from sustainably managed forests. Soy-based inks were used in its printing and
the laminate film is biodegradable.

A catalogue record for this book is available from the British Library

Printed in Singapore by Craft Print International Ltd

Walking with
Gospel Women

INTERACTIVE BIBLE MEDITATIONS

FIONA STRATTA

Contents

Introduction

The following monologues and studies are based on the biblical accounts of women found in the Gospels and are intended for groups of women who meet together in order to grow in their relationships with God and each other. The group should first read the Bible passage about the woman to be studied, followed by the monologue, which is written as if the woman herself is speaking.

There are several types of Christian meditation, one of which is to 'enter' the scripture using the imagination. Imaginative reflection on the Bible is not a new concept; it was practised by St Ignatius of Loyola in the 16th century.

Emilie Griffin wrote:

> Meditation is… a work of the graced imagination. Understand first that imagination is one of God's great gifts to us and has a vital place in the spiritual life. Meditation allows us to put godly imagination into play in such a way that our faith feels more alive. Often this practice allows Scripture to work in us more effectively.[1]

Imaginative meditation can be a refreshing and powerful way for God to speak to us, for it involves not only the mind but also the emotions. Jesus himself used imaginative narrative in the form of parables to engage with his listeners and hence to teach them effectively. In these studies we are to cast ourselves as the women in the Gospel episodes.

Of course, not everything in the monologues will be true. After all, we are imagining, filling in the gaps with possibilities. This need not be a problem, for it is precisely what we do when we tell Bible stories to children: we embellish the story to capture the child's imagination, with the purpose of teaching them spiritual truths. This is exactly what we are doing here.

Points for reflection and discussion follow the monologues, enabling issues to be explored and spiritual growth to take place. 'Man's chief end is to glorify God and to enjoy him forever'[2] and so each reflection and discussion ends by considering how the study has contributed to our growing relationship with God as Father, Son and Holy Spirit.

Finally, there is the opportunity to record what God has been saying to us and the implications for our individual spiritual journeys. After all, in coming to God's word, we want not only to learn but also to change and to grow, so that we are 'doers of the word, and not merely hearers' (James 1:22, NRSV).

The monologues can be used in groups without the discussion element as a means of initiating a time of silent personal reflection or led meditation. The monologues can also stand alone effectively in many other contexts: for example, individuals can use them in private meditation or the monologues can be read to larger groups such as congregations.

The facilitator

You will need to ensure that pens and paper and a variety of translations and paraphrases of the Bible are available for the group. For the longer studies, you may need to select the passages to be read and the questions to be discussed.

It will be your responsibility to introduce the study and to find someone to read the monologue. Try to ask someone who is able to read aloud fluently and expressively.

You will need to read out the links and facilitate the discussion, allowing enough time for personal reflection at the end. It may be helpful to play quiet music while this last part is happening.

Elizabeth

Introduction

- Read Luke 1:5–25, 39–45 and 57–80. The first two references could be read before the monologue and the final one afterwards.

- Ask God to speak to you through this episode. You could use the words from Psalm 119:18: 'Open my eyes to see wonderful things in your Word' (LB).

- Sit back, relax and close your eyes. Imagine the scene as someone reads out the monologue.

Monologue

Zechariah had been gone for a week and I was expecting him home that day. My husband was a member of the priestly family of Abijah and had gone to Jerusalem to fulfil his week of duty at the temple. It was such an important week, for Zechariah was meticulous in his obedience to the Lord's commands and regulations and he found great satisfaction in his priestly responsibilities. He would be tired after his journey back to the hill country of Judea where we lived, for we were elderly now and the spell of temple service took its toll on him. I went to the doorway from time to time to look out for him. At last there he was, walking toward me, but to my astonishment his walk was brisk and his face animated. I welcomed him but he made no reply as he took me into his arms and smiled broadly.

As we entered our home I started to ply him with questions: How had it been? Who had he seen? What was the news from Jerusalem? Who had been chosen to enter the sanctuary of the Lord to burn the incense on behalf of the people?

Still silence from my husband and still that smile, and when I looked into his eyes there was an expression that I had never seen before. I couldn't make it out. My questions dried up and my excitement was replaced with concern. I couldn't get a word out of him! What was the matter? Zechariah was scanning the room, looking for something. Then his eyes fell on the writing tablet and, with a look of relief, he walked over and brought it back to where I stood. He drew me to his side and wrote the words, 'We will have a son and we will call him John.'

I sat down with a thump. What was happening? Had he gone mad? We were old, we were childless—a great pain to us both—and now I was well past the age of conceiving a baby.

Slowly and painstakingly the story began to unfold. With a trembling hand Zechariah continued to write and I tried to interpret what had happened, while he nodded or shook his head. This is what I pieced together.

My husband had been chosen by lot to enter the sanctuary to burn incense while the crowd stayed outside, praying. In the sanctuary the angel Gabriel had appeared to him, giving him the momentous message that we were to have a son and his name was to be John. He would be a joy and delight to us, his birth would cause many to rejoice and he would be great in the eyes of the Lord. From his very birth he would be filled with the Holy Spirit and be consecrated to God: he was set aside for a special purpose. He would bring people back to the Lord, turning them round from disobedience to righteous living and preparing them for the coming of the Lord. Our son would have the spirit and power of Elijah!

God was once again moving in Israel. After years of waiting and seeming silence, the promise made through the prophet Malachi was going to be fulfilled: 'Look, I am sending you the prophet Elijah before the great and dreadful day of the Lord arrives. His preaching will turn the hearts of fathers to their children, and the hearts of children to their fathers.'[3]

There were two things we had longed for, had prayed for, all our lives: to have a child and for the coming of the Redeemer of Israel. Yet when an angel was sent to tell Zechariah that our longings were to be fulfilled, he could not believe it. I couldn't blame him, for this was beyond anything we had imagined. So Zechariah had been struck dumb, had been unable to say those words that the people were longing to hear when he came out of the sanctuary: 'The Lord bless you and keep you; the Lord make his face shine upon you and be gracious to you; the Lord turn his face toward you and give you peace.'[4]

My husband had signed to them and the people had realised that he'd seen a vision. How hard it had been for him to complete his duties, for he was longing to return to me. But in the quietness his hope and faith had grown, and by the time I saw him there was not a flicker of doubt in his eyes. I believed.

Zechariah's love-making was tender that night and I knew, before there was any indication, that I was pregnant. For five months I remained secluded, preparing myself to be the mother of this man of God. I thought of his name, John: 'the Lord is gracious'. That was God's message to us and to all his people, the message that our son would take to them. How carefully we must prepare him for his role.

In the sixth month of my pregnancy I was absorbed in sweeping the house when I heard the simple words, 'Hello, Elizabeth.'

Oh! My son leapt within my womb. I turned and there was my young cousin, Mary. I knew immediately, without her uttering a further word. I knew that she was pregnant and I knew that the baby she carried was the Chosen One. God's Spirit so filled me that I could not but call out, 'You are blessed among women! Blessed too is the child you will bear! I am so favoured that the mother of the Lord should visit me. As soon as you called my name, my baby leapt for joy. You are blessed for believing that the Lord will accomplish what he has promised.'.

I listened as Mary praised God, as her beautiful words filled our home: 'My soul glorifies the Lord and my spirit rejoices in God my Saviour.'[5]

Mary spent three months with me. We had much to share and we drew much strength from this time together. I helped her through those early weeks of pregnancy and she helped me with practical matters in the home as I became more fatigued. I was sad to see her go, but return to her home she must and I must prepare myself for the birth.

It was both the most difficult and the most joyful day of my life, giving birth to my son. I remember the delight of holding him in my arms and seeing Zechariah's pride and pleasure. Our joy was increased by our family and friends, who rejoiced with us and joined us for the circumcision and naming on the eighth day of our son's life.

During the ceremony I realised that the rabbi was referring to our son as Zechariah. 'No!' I interrupted. 'His name is to be John.'

Everyone looked at me in great surprise. 'But no one in

your family has the name John,' they argued. I looked at Zechariah and a writing tablet was brought to him. Silence fell on the crowd as he wrote, 'His name is John.'

As soon as he held this up for all to see, my husband began to speak. The Spirit of God filled him and he spoke words of praise and prophecy for everyone to hear, words from the scriptures that we were familiar with and loved to hear, for they promised us a future. This time was different, though, for now the words spoke of the present and not of a time to come: 'He has come and has redeemed his people. He has raised up a horn of salvation for us... You, my child, will be called a prophet of the Most High.'[6]

I looked around the faces of our friends and family as they listened to Zechariah; they were full of wonder. As they left, I heard them talking quietly to each other about the future of our son. Was not the Lord's hand on him in a special way?

Reflection and discussion

- Did any words or phrases stand out for you? Before further discussion, read some or all of the passages again in a different translation or paraphrase of the Bible.

- Zechariah and Elizabeth lived faithfully in spite of ongoing difficult circumstances and heartache. The Bible passage states that they were 'righteous in God's eyes' (v. 6). How can we live faithfully and with integrity in challenging circumstances?

- From a human perspective, it is easy to understand Zechariah's doubts. We can fall into the trap of trusting in our own reason and logic rather than in God. The experiences that we have had, especially bad ones, can limit our ability to expect great things from God in the future and can cause us to live in a less hopeful and more cynical way. They can take away the song from our hearts. Share experiences of this loss of hopefulness.

■ Cynical unbelief is seen as a very serious condition in this passage: not only was the song taken from Zechariah's heart but he was also dumb for nine months. Our faith and trust may seem inadequate but we are assured that we need only have faith the size of a mustard seed to do great things in God's name (Matthew 17:20–21). Share times when you have seen God at work although your faith at that moment was small.

■ Elizabeth had carried a great burden because of the false beliefs about childlessness held at that time and the unhelpful attitudes of the people around her. We can be burdened by false pictures of God or ideas about Christian living that have been passed down to us, or we may unwittingly burden others. Share your experiences of this.

■ Elizabeth's life of humiliation was to be changed to one of great blessing, for John was to be a joy and delight to her. We read in Romans 8:28, 'And we know that God causes everything to work together for the good of those who love God and are called according to his purpose for them.' Share how God has done this in your lives. Are there painful areas in your lives from which you would like God to bring good? You may feel unable to share them openly but it may be helpful to write them down in your personal reflections at the end of the session.

■ Jesus would later refer to John as the greatest of all children born to women (Luke 7:28). The story of Elizabeth encourages us never to lose hope: God will sometimes surprise us with his intervention. Are there times in your life when God has intervened in surprising and wonderful ways?

- 'Elizabeth became pregnant and went into seclusion for five months' (Luke 1:24). Quietness can provide a time for spiritual growth; the noise around us can block our receptivity to God and to what he is saying. For this reason many Christians build quiet days and/or silent retreats into their schedules. If this sounds daunting, start with a couple of hours. Those in the group who have experienced such times of quietness could share the value gained from seeking silence.

- Elizabeth describes Mary as blessed for believing God's promises. We can live in deep peace in all kinds of situations as we learn to live with the simple trust that God is in control and will fulfil his promises to us. Share times when holding on to a biblical promise has given you peace.

- Zechariah was unable to say this blessing when he came out of the sanctuary: 'The Lord bless you and keep you; the Lord make his face shine on you and be gracious to you; the Lord turn his face toward you and give you peace' (Numbers 6:24–26, NIV). It is a wonderful blessing to pray over and for those we know and love. Say this blessing to each other at the end of your time together.

- John, Elizabeth and Zechariah are all described in these passages as filled with the Holy Spirit. What have you learnt of the work of the Holy Spirit through this study?

Conclusion

Take time to pray through your findings. What might God be saying to you? Is anything particularly relevant to your life at the moment? Write down what you have learnt and refer back to it regularly in the days ahead so that it becomes part of your thinking, reacting and lifestyle.

Mary: the annunciation

Introduction

- Read Luke 1:26–38.

- Ask God to speak to you through this episode. You could use the words from Psalm 119:27: 'Help me understand these things inside and out so I can ponder your miracle-wonders' (*THE MESSAGE*).

- Sit back, relax and close your eyes. Imagine the scene as someone reads out the monologue.

Monologue

A constant song seemed to fill my heart in those days, one of great happiness. I was a young woman with so much to look forward to, for I was recently betrothed to a fine man, Joseph, a descendant of David. Joseph was a carpenter and whenever he had a spare moment he would work on building a home for us; I watched his progress with delight. One day I remember asking him what he thought about as he worked, and he had answered quite simply, 'I pray.'

As I walked to collect water from the well in Nazareth, I would daydream, imagining our wedding celebrations, our life together, the children I would bear. How happy I would be! I, too, prayed as I worked, asking that God would be my strength, that I would be a good wife and a loving mother, bringing up my children in the ways of the Lord. I thanked God for Joseph and asked God to bless our life together. In my heart I would repeat words from the psalm:

'Blessed are they whose ways are blameless, who walk according to the law of the Lord. Blessed are they who keep his statutes and seek him with all their heart... I have hidden your word in my heart that I might not sin against you... I rejoice in following your statutes as one rejoices in great riches. I meditate on your precepts and consider your ways. I delight in your decrees; I will not neglect your word.'[7]

It was a day like any other and I was humming to myself when I entered the house. It would usually take a few moments for my eyes to adapt to the dark interior after the bright sunshine outside, but that day it was brighter within, intensely bright. I put the waterpot down and instinctively covered my eyes with my hands. I sensed the light getting closer to me and felt a strange warmth course through my body. Then I heard a voice and, in fear, I fell to the ground.

'Greetings, you who are highly favoured! The Lord is with you.'

Who was this speaking to me? Why these words? I was finding it difficult to breathe, my hands trembled violently and my body shook. The beautifully resonant voice spoke again: 'I am Gabriel, sent by God. Do not be afraid, Mary; you have found favour with God. You will conceive and give birth to a son. You are to give him the name Jesus.'

The realisation swept over me: this was a heavenly being before me, an angel of the Lord. My trembling hands fell away from my face, my fear started to subside and into its place seeped a deep awe. There was a long silence, and the warmth and light seemed to penetrate my very soul. The quietness was broken by the words, 'He will be great and will be called the Son of the Most High. The Lord God will give him the throne of his father David, and he will reign over the house of Jacob for ever; his kingdom will never end.'[8]

'How can this be?' I faltered. 'I have never slept with a man.'

'The Holy Spirit will come upon you, and the power of the Most High will overshadow you. So the holy one to be born will be called the Son of God.'[9]

Light and warmth hovered around me, shone over me, washed me, pierced me, softened me and opened me to receive these promises.

The angel spoke again: 'Even your relative, Elizabeth, has conceived in her old age and is now six months pregnant. For nothing is impossible with God.'

'I am the Lord's servant. May everything you have said about me come true,'[10] I responded. Darkness descended as the light faded and I was left alone.

Reflection and discussion

- Did any words or phrases stand out for you? Before further discussion, read the passage again in a different translation or paraphrase of the Bible.

- In the monologue, Mary and Joseph both prayed as they worked. The 17th-century monk, Brother Lawrence, who worked in a busy kitchen, learnt to 'practise the presence of God' while at work. How could we build an awareness of God's presence into our daily lives?

- The words that Mary is imagined to meditate on come from Psalm 119:1–2, 11 and 14–16 (NIV). In verse 11 we read the words, 'I have hidden your word in my heart that I might not sin against you.' How can we 'hide' God's word in our hearts?

- Angels are God's messengers and appear on many occasions during the Christmas story, as well as elsewhere in the Bible, from Genesis to Revelation. Encounters with angels have continued throughout history to the modern day. Which angel appearances to humans can you recall from the Bible?

■ Sometimes angels are sent to give a specific message from God, and on other occasions they come to give protection. What historical or modern-day stories of angels have you heard? We are told that these messengers of God will not necessarily take on an angelic countenance: 'Don't forget to show hospitality to strangers, for some who have done this have entertained angels without realising it!' (Hebrews 13:2).

■ Mary was open to receive from God, as her final words illustrate: 'I am the Lord's servant. May everything you have said about me come true' (Luke 1:38). Jesus spoke of people having hard hearts that prevented them from receiving and responding to his word. We are warned against this in Hebrews 3:7–8: 'The Holy Spirit says, "Today when you hear his voice, don't harden your hearts as Israel did when they rebelled, when they tested me in the wilderness".' Our hearts can become hardened so that we do not respond in compassion to people, hardened so that we see no other doctrinal view but our own and hardened so that we do not see God's blessing in our lives. Share other ways in which our hearts can become hardened and give specific examples where possible. We need to pray daily for softened hearts so that we can respond to the Spirit of God.

■ Mary was told that the Holy Spirit would come upon her. Luke recognises the work of the Holy Spirit throughout his accounts of the life of Jesus and of the early church. Mary would need the indwelling Spirit to sustain her and give her wisdom in all that lay ahead. Jesus likens the Holy Spirit to the wind (John 3:5–8). The wind can be the most gentle and refreshing of breezes or a powerful gale. In the same way, our experiences of the Holy Spirit's activity can vary greatly. Give examples from your own lives.

■ The angel told Mary that nothing is impossible with God. Share times when God has worked in seemingly impossible circumstances in your life or in the lives of people you know. You may have 'impossible' situations that you are dealing with at the moment. If you are able, share them with the group, and bring them to God in your time of individual reflection at the end.

■ At the end of this episode, the angel leaves Mary. Our times of revelation and insight, deep fellowship and joyful celebration are wonderful but are not continuous. The Bible tells us that Mary 'treasured up all these things and pondered them in her heart' (Luke 2:19, NIV). It is likely that the memory of this event and the confirmation from Elizabeth helped to sustain her. Share how you have been sustained in difficult times by the memory of God's blessings.

■ 'The Lord is with you!' (Luke 1:28). This message is at the heart of the Christmas story. These words to Mary are also God's words to us. How does this affect our relationship with God?

Conclusion

Take time to pray through your findings. What might God be saying to you? Is anything particularly relevant to your life at the moment? Write down what you have learnt and refer back to it regularly in the days ahead so that it becomes part of your thinking, reacting and lifestyle.

Mary's visit to Elizabeth

Introduction

■ Read Luke 1:39–56.

■ Ask God to speak to you through this episode. You could use the words from Psalm 119:144: 'The way you tell me to live is always right; help me understand it so I can live to the fullest' (THE MESSAGE).

■ Sit back, relax and close your eyes. Imagine the scene as someone reads out the monologue.

Monologue

The next few days I was in turmoil. How could I tell my parents? How could I tell Joseph? Would anyone believe me? What would my neighbours say? What would become of me when Joseph knew that I was pregnant? Would my parents reject me? I could not bring myself to say a word and yet I knew by their anxious glances that they sensed my strain. I craved space and quiet, wanting to think about the words of the angel. I had been told that Elizabeth was expecting a child. The confirmation I needed was Elizabeth.

Eventually I sought out my mother. 'I would like to go and stay with Elizabeth for a few weeks,' I blurted out, not wanting to be asked any questions.

With a surprised look my mother said, 'Elizabeth? When were you thinking of going?'

'I want to leave early tomorrow. Please don't ask me why.

I need to see her. And please tell Joseph that I will be back in a few weeks. I will talk to him then.'

I hugged my mother and a tear rolled down my cheek, which I brushed away hurriedly, not wanting her to see my pain. How could I do this to Joseph—leave him without a word of explanation? But I had to go. I had to see Elizabeth.

So it was that I made the journey into the hill country of Judea, to the home of Zechariah and Elizabeth. What a torrent of thoughts whirled around my head as I travelled! I knew that one look at Elizabeth would be enough to reassure me.

At last I stood at her door, my heart thumping wildly. I entered and there was my cousin. My eyes dropped down immediately from her face to her body. Oh, there was no denying it! There was life there, blossoming within her. Joy flooded my soul and I stretched out my hands to take hers. But Elizabeth was looking at me intently, searching my face. She gave a gasp, put one hand on to her swollen belly and put her other hand in mine. Her words of greeting astounded me, for she knew. Although I had only just conceived this holy babe, she knew of him. My cousin recognised that the peasant girl before her was to be the mother of the Lord.

'God has blessed you above all women, and your child is blessed,' I heard her say. 'Why am I so honoured, that the mother of my Lord should visit me? When I heard your greeting, the baby in my womb jumped for joy. You are blessed because you believed that the Lord would do what he said.'[11]

My spirit soared and my heart was filled with such joy that I could not keep silent.

> 'Oh, how my soul praises the Lord.
> How my spirit rejoices in God my Saviour!

For he took notice of his lowly servant girl,
and from now on all generations will call me blessed.
For the Mighty One is holy,
and he has done great things for me.
He shows mercy from generation to generation
to all who fear him.
His mighty arm has done tremendous things!
He has scattered the proud and the haughty ones.
He has brought down princes from their thrones
and exalted the humble.
He has filled the hungry with good things
and sent the rich away with empty hands.
He has helped his servant Israel
and remembered to be merciful.
For he made this promise to our ancestors,
to Abraham and his children forever.'[12]

How precious were those days with Elizabeth! I learnt much from her wise words, and her encouragement strengthened me for the days ahead when I would have to return to Nazareth.

Reflection and discussion

- Did any words or phrases stand out for you? Before further discussion, read the passage again in a different translation or paraphrase of the Bible.

- Mary believes the angel but receives confirmation of the angel's words by visiting Elizabeth and seeing that she is pregnant. There may have been occasions when you have believed and then received confirmation from God, perhaps through another person, which has filled you with confidence and gladness. Share any of these occasions.

- Mary's song of praise is known as the Magnificat and has had an important place in Christian worship throughout the generations. In our prayers, how can we, like Mary, focus on the greatness of God, his faithfulness, his justice, his promises and his goodness to us? Prayers of this nature affirm our faith and help us to live our lives in humble gratitude to God. We can echo the words of Mary: 'For the Mighty One is holy, and he has done great things for me' (Luke 1:49).

- These would have been challenging days for Mary and the friendship and advice of an older and spiritually more mature woman would have been invaluable to her. Have you been helped through the wisdom of a friend or through a more formally arranged spiritual friendship or mentor? In what ways? Have you been supported by someone who is going or has gone through similar experiences to yours? How?

- Mary was 'blessed above all women' and clearly in the will of God, but her obedience was to be very costly from the moment she said 'yes' to God. The spiritual life brings joy, peace and blessing but also can be full of anguish as the Holy Spirit transforms us at the core of our beings and as we walk in obedience to God. Can you recount any times in your life when following God took you in a direction that proved to be difficult, even though you were sure you were taking the right course of action? Share your thoughts. Many Christian writers have told of such times in their lives, which have resulted in eventual blessing for them and for others. Encourage your group with any stories you have heard.

- What have you learnt of God the Father and his dealings with us from this episode?

Conclusion

Take time to pray through your findings. What might God be saying to you? Is anything particularly relevant to your life at the moment? Write down what you have learnt and refer back to it regularly in the days ahead so that it becomes part of your thinking, reacting and lifestyle.

Mary and the birth of Christ

Introduction

- Read Matthew 1:18–25 and Luke 2:1–20.

- Ask God to speak to you through this episode. You could use the words from Psalm 119:169: 'Let my cry come right into your presence, God; provide me with the insight that comes only from your Word' (THE MESSAGE).

- Sit back, relax and close your eyes. Imagine the scene as someone reads out the monologue.

Monologue

They were long, hard days for a heavily pregnant woman, those three days of journeying from Nazareth to Bethlehem. Sometimes I walked for a while, but most of the time I sat on our donkey's back, trying to smile at Joseph when he threw me anxious glances, my thoughts filled with the events of the last few months. Who could imagine that life could change so quickly?

In the weeks that followed my return from Elizabeth's home, I had needed the memory of the peace and joy I had experienced with her. There had been the agony of telling my parents that I was expecting a child, the pain of bearing their words of disbelief as I told them my story. More difficult still had been telling Joseph, seeing the devastation in his eyes. Fear had gripped me, fear not just for myself but also for the child within me: I knew that Joseph had every right to have me stoned to death. How could I have ever thought that he would believe me? I remembered hearing him in earnest conversation with my father, seeing my father's look of relief as he came out to my mother and me, telling us that Joseph did not wish me harm, not even public disgrace, but would end the betrothal quietly.

In the weeks ahead, I stayed inside, not wishing to face the accusing eyes of the other women. There was no longer the possibility of hiding the baby I carried, for the bulge of his growing body was beginning to show. My parents bore the brunt of the shame, for they heard the cruel rumours; they were ignored; the respect that they deserved was lost. They were dark days. Yet at the same time I felt the wonder of this child growing within me, the joy of feeling his first kick, the amazement that I had been chosen to carry the Son of God.

I remembered the evening when Joseph had astonished us by reappearing at our house. He looked tired and haggard, insisting that he needed to talk to us. His words were to transform all of our lives, because he described to us a dream in which he had been visited by an angel.

'What did the angel say?' I whispered.

'That I should not be afraid to take you as my wife, Mary. That all you have said is true: the baby within you is conceived by the Holy Spirit. That you are to have a son and we should call him Jesus, for he will save his people from their sins.'

We all cried with relief. I had so many reasons to be grateful to this man who was willing to support me and the child I was to bear, to provide for us both. Every day I gave thanks to God for revealing his plan to Joseph.

I remembered the day when news reached Nazareth that a census had been called by Caesar Augustus. Everyone was to return to his home town to register. Joseph, being a descendant of David, was to go to Bethlehem and, as I was pledged to him in marriage, I had to go too. It was not a good time to make a journey: I was so near to the end of my pregnancy. My mother anxiously did all she could to prepare me for the birth, giving me instructions, helping me to pack salt and strips of swaddling cloth in which to wrap my son. But in spite of my fears, a part of me was glad to leave the prying eyes and gossip of our neighbours.

As we journeyed and I relived these events in my mind, my tiredness grew with every mile. Then, on our final day's journey, I noticed them—the tightenings, weak at first, but always growing stronger and more persistent. Joseph assured me that we were nearly there; soon I would have help.

We entered Bethlehem as afternoon turned to evening. The town was heaving with people. In the noise and bustle and now with regular, intense contractions, waves of panic started to flood over me. On the edge of my consciousness I was aware of Joseph asking for a place for us to stay, over and over again, but always receiving the same answer: 'No room.' Surely God's Son was not to be born on the street?

The next thing I was aware of was being led by a woman into her small house to the tiny guest area above the animals' living quarters.

That was where the Son of God was born. As, at last, I held him, such love for this tiny infant filled me to overflowing. We wrapped him in the swaddling cloths and laid him in the manger, for there was no other space in the house. I lay back exhausted on the blankets that Joseph had laid out for me.

'Is this really what you intended for the coming of your Son into the world?' I mused.

Joseph was kneeling next to the manger, looking intently

at our baby. 'Jesus', I heard him say. 'But you, O Bethlehem Ephrathah, are only a small village among all the people of Judah. Yet a ruler of Israel will come from you, one whose origins are from the distant past,'[13] he murmured. I shut my eyes and started to doze.

I was awakened by the noise of the door being opened. Joseph jumped up and stood protectively between the men who entered and baby Jesus. They were unkempt, rough-looking men. Joseph asked them what they wanted. They were shepherds, they said, out in the fields near Bethlehem, keeping their flock safe from night-time dangers. Suddenly the sky had lit up and an angel of the Lord had appeared to them. They were terrified and fell to the ground.

Then the angel had spoken: 'Do not be afraid. I am bringing you good news that is for all people. The Saviour, the Messiah, the Lord has been born today in Bethlehem, the city of David. You will know you have found him when you find a baby wrapped in cloth and lying in a manger.'

The angel was joined by a crowd of angels until the sky was filled with their beauty and music, praising God: 'Glory to God in highest heaven, and peace on earth to those with whom God is pleased.'[14] Then it went dark and the silence of the night returned.

'Let's go to Bethlehem and see this baby that the Lord had told us about,' the shepherds had said to one another. So they had stumbled their way into the town in the darkness and eventually found us and everything exactly as they had been told by the angel.

I called them forward and they came and marvelled at the beauty and perfection of the baby before them. Their excitement filled my soul. This day that had, at moments, seemed so out of control had been lovingly watched over by God. He had confirmed his promise to me yet again, this time through the shepherds.

They went on their way filled with joy and praising God. In the days that followed, the shepherds told everyone they met about what they had seen and heard. The people who heard were amazed, but I wondered whether they would remember the shepherds' story in years to come.

I did. I often thought about their words. There are some things so precious, so close to our hearts. We think of them often but speak of them seldom.

Reflection and discussion

- Did any words or phrases stand out for you? Before further discussion, read the passage again in a different translation or paraphrase of the Bible.

- The course of Mary's life changed very quickly. Have there been times in your life when your circumstances have changed quickly? If you can, share your stories. Adapting to change can be a challenge, but we have the promise that 'Jesus Christ is the same yesterday, today, and forever' (Hebrews 13:8) and the words of Jesus, 'And be sure of this: I am with you always, even to the end of the age' (Matthew 28:20).

- Their God-given responsibility to nurture Jesus must have given Mary and Joseph a great sense of purpose in their lives. Although there is a deep sense of satisfaction in the knowledge that we are fulfilling God's purposes for our lives, life can also be difficult because of the challenges of going against the norms of our surrounding culture. Joseph may well have been a figure of ridicule for taking Mary as his wife rather than following the expected practice of his day. Have there been times when, because of your faith, you have taken steps that have been counter-cultural? What were the outcomes?

- Joseph demonstrated not only immediate obedience to the angel of the Lord but also courage and humility. Have you seen these characteristics combined in those wanting to walk in a close and obedient relationship to God?

- Many prophecies about the coming Messiah were fulfilled through the events surrounding the birth of Jesus Christ. We see the sovereignty of God in the amazing timing of the Roman census, which meant that Joseph and Mary were in Bethlehem for the birth of Jesus. It can be faith-strengthening to look at the details revealed to the prophets by God hundreds of years before the birth of Christ. In your own time, you may like to look at the following: the king who will be a descendant of David (Jeremiah 23:5); the virgin birth (Isaiah 7:14); the birthplace (Micah 5:2); the visit from eastern men with their gifts (Psalm 72:10); the massacre of the babies (Jeremiah 31:15) and the return of Jesus from Egypt (Hosea 11:1).

- It must have been hard for Mary to hold on to the prom-ises of God when she arrived in Bethlehem and gave birth in such difficult circumstances. Share experiences of times when you've had to hold on to promises even when the evidence before you seemed to deny those promises.

- The animals' living area is an unlikely place for the Son of God to be placed to sleep but it made him approachable and accessible to the poor of the world. God's heart is for the poor. Read Jesus' words in Matthew 5:3, 5: 'God blesses those who are poor and realise their need for him, for the Kingdom of Heaven is theirs... God blesses those who are humble, for they will inherit the whole earth.' How can we share God's heart for the poor?

- Shepherds were lowly people. Are we in danger of making Jesus inaccessible to some people by our behaviour and traditions?
- What in this episode has given you a better understanding of God the Father and his plans for humanity?

Conclusion

Take time to pray through your findings. What might God be saying to you? Is anything particularly relevant to your life at the moment? Write down what you have learnt and refer back to it regularly in the days ahead so that it becomes part of your thinking, reacting and lifestyle.

Anna the prophetess

Introduction

- Read Luke 2:21–38.

- Ask God to speak to you through this episode. You could use the words from Psalm 119:41: 'May your unfailing love come to me, Lord, your salvation according to your promise' (NIV).

- Sit back, relax and close your eyes. Imagine the scene as someone reads out the monologue.

Monologue

Those short, seven years of marriage seemed like a hazy memory to me by the time I was in my 84th year. The law made provision for me and insisted on the inclusion of widows in our religious celebrations; for that I was grateful. However, I still often found myself overlooked and this added to the pain of losing my fine young husband and finding myself alone at what should have been the prime of life. I started to take deep comfort from the words of the Psalms: 'Father to the fatherless, defender of widows—this is God, whose dwelling is holy'[15] and 'The Lord protects the foreigners among us. He cares for the orphans and widows.'[16]

Slowly I realised that, while God had a great love for the nation of Israel, he loved and watched over those individuals who sought his ways; he cared deeply about *me*. With time I experienced the truth of the words, 'He heals the broken-hearted and bandages their wounds.'[17]

There were so many worries and concerns in those early days but, with each day that passed, I learnt to cast my cares and burdens on the Lord. As I discovered more of God's love for me, I grew to love him more, as a wife loves a husband who treats her with tenderness. I would go as far as saying that God was a husband to me, for the holy Scriptures say, 'Your Creator will be your husband; the Lord of Heaven's Armies is his name! He is your Redeemer, the Holy One of Israel, the God of all the earth.'[18]

I understood that a woman who no longer has a husband will be loved tenderly by God, 'For the Lord has called you back from your grief—as though you were a young wife abandoned by her husband.'[19]

How precious were these words to me! I desired nothing so much as to be worshipping my God, singing praises to him and understanding his ways. That is how I came to spend more and more time in the temple: I was often there day and night, praying and fasting.

The days rolled into years and, with their passing, I had a growing expectation that God was going to visit his people. Our nation was living through terrible times of oppression and, for so long, it had seemed that God was silent. But I clung to the words of Malachi the prophet that 'the Sun of Righteousness will rise with healing in his wings'.[20]

I was not alone in this belief. Simeon, like me, belonged to the remnant waiting for the 'consolation of Israel', as he put it. The Holy Spirit had revealed to Simeon, who was now late in years, that he would not die until he had seen the Lord's Messiah. So we waited.

We were not to be disappointed. One day I was walking across the Court of Women at the temple when I saw Simeon in earnest conversation with a young couple. The woman was holding her baby close to her; a look of such tender love appeared on her face whenever she looked down at the child. The man, considerably older than his wife, seemed strong and capable and would glance protectively first at his wife and then at the child. No doubt the family had come for their ceremony of purification according to the law of Moses.

There was a look of ecstatic joy on Simeon's old face and I felt a stirring within me as I drew near to them. I heard Simeon's words as he took the child in his arms and praised God: 'Sovereign Lord, as you have promised, you now dismiss your servant in peace. For my eyes have seen your salvation, which you have prepared in the sight of all people, a light for revelation to the Gentiles and for glory to your people Israel.'[21] The child's parents looked at each other with wonder in their eyes. It seemed to me that, although marvelling at this declaration, they seemed to understand something of the enormity of Simeon's words. Did they already know that their child was the long-awaited One? Praise God! My heart filled with joy and thanksgiving, for he had visited his people, just as he had promised.

I watched as Simeon blessed the child and then handed him to his mother. There was a pause as Simeon studied the woman's face. Then he spoke to her with a measured tone and great solemnity: 'This child is destined to cause the falling and rising of many in Israel, and to be a sign that will be spoken against, so that the thoughts of many hearts will be revealed. And a sword will pierce your own soul too.'[22] A shadow passed across the young woman's face, but she said nothing.

I approached the family with arms outstretched, praising God for remembering his people, for sending our Redeemer. So we worshipped God together and then they left the temple to return to Bethlehem, for that is where the baby had been born.

From that day I took up my God's instruction to console his people and to proclaim his truth: '"Comfort, comfort my people," says your God. "Speak tenderly to Jerusalem. Tell her that her sad days are gone and her sins are pardoned."'[23]

I told all who would listen about the child, explaining to those who came to the temple and were looking forward to the redemption of Israel that the time had come, 'For to us a child is born, to us a son is given, and the government will be on his shoulders. And he will be called Wonderful Counsellor, Mighty God, Everlasting Father, Prince of Peace.'[24]

Reflection and discussion

- Did any words or phrases stand out for you? Before further discussion, read the passage again in a different translation or paraphrase of the Bible.

- We have imagined that Anna journeyed from a general understanding of God's love for the people of Israel to a specific understanding of God's love for her. If you are able, share how you have made or are making this journey yourself.

- In the monologue Anna had learnt to 'cast her cares on the Lord' daily. Read Psalm 55:22: 'Cast your cares on the Lord and he will sustain you' (NIV). In what ways can we give our burdens to God? How can we learn to live one day at a time? Jesus teaches us, 'Therefore do not worry about tomorrow, for tomorrow will worry about itself' (Matthew 6:34, NIV). In your own time at home, meditate on Matthew 6:25–34.

- Anna saw God as her husband both because of her intimacy with him and because of his provision for her, quoting from Isaiah 54:5: 'Your Creator will be your husband.' How do you respond to this idea? The picture is carried through into the New Testament, where the Church is portrayed as the bride of Christ.

- Life's circumstances can make us bitter or better. Anna chose to draw close to God and receive his consolation. Our heavenly Father is always seeking us out, longing to console us. James says, 'Come near to God and he will come near to you.' (James 4:8 NIV). Anna is imagined to quote from Psalm 147:3: 'He heals the broken-hearted and binds up their wounds' (NIV). If you are able, share your experiences of God being your consolation.

- In Simeon, Anna discovered a like-minded person—someone who was also seeking to walk closely with the Lord and had the same prophetic vision. Have you been particularly encouraged by a like-minded person? Simeon said that Jesus was 'destined to cause the falling and rising of many in Israel'. It is thought that this refers to the prophecy in Isaiah 8:14, 'He will be a stone that makes people stumble, a rock that makes them fall.'

- Jesus made such incredible claims about himself that it was not and is not an option to remain neutral about him. For example, he said, 'I am the light of the world' (John 9:5, NIV). What other claims did he make? Jesus could not have been 'just a good man': either he was all he claimed to be or he was a liar, a madman or even possessed. If time permits, read Mark 3:20–30. The responses that individuals made to Jesus resulted in their 'falling or rising'. Today we still have to answer the question that Jesus asked his disciples: 'Who do you say I am?' (Luke 9:20, NIV). Ask some group members to describe their journey to belief in Jesus as the Messiah, the Son of God.

- Simeon was led by the Holy Spirit to the temple courts where he met Mary and Joseph with Jesus. The words that he was inspired to say were both words of blessing and words of challenge. Have you been called on to give words of blessing or challenge, or been on the receiving end of words of blessing or challenge? Share your experiences.

- Anna was elderly but she received a new assignment from God: 'She talked about the child to everyone who had been waiting expectantly for God to rescue Jerusalem' (Luke 2:38). Like Anna, whatever age we have reached, God has purposes for us. Age never takes us beyond God's care: 'Even to your old age and grey hairs I am he, I am he who will sustain you. I have made you and I will carry you; I will sustain you and I will rescue you' (Isaiah 46:4, NIV).

- Our spiritual journey continues to the very end of our lives if we are open to God's renewing work within us and to new assignments and purpose that he gives us. 'Therefore we do not lose heart. Though outwardly we are wasting away, yet inwardly we are being renewed day by day' (2 Corinthians 4:16, NIV). Do you know elderly people whose lives demonstrate the truth of these verses? How is the spiritual contribution of the elderly valued in your Christian community?

- In this episode we see God the Father's plan unfold, we get a foretaste of the ministry of Christ and we see the Holy Spirit working in the lives of Simeon and Anna. How has this helped you to know God more?

Conclusion

Take time to pray through your findings. What might God be saying to you? Is anything particularly relevant to your life at the moment? Write down what you have learnt and refer back to it regularly in the days ahead so that it becomes part of your thinking, reacting and lifestyle.

Mary and the child Jesus

Introduction

- Read Matthew 2:1–23 and Luke 2:51–52.

- Ask God to speak to you through this episode. You could use the words from Psalm 119:135: 'Smile on me, your servant; teach me the right way to live' (*THE MESSAGE*).

- Sit back, relax and close your eyes. Imagine the scene as someone reads out the monologue.

Monologue

Those first months in Jesus' life were so precious to me. I delighted in the progress he made—the first smile, his gurgles and first sounds, the first tottering steps towards me, his growing interest in the plants, the animals and the people surrounding our house in Bethlehem.

Joseph had found a home for us after Jesus' birth and since then he had worked as a carpenter. We had settled into a peaceful routine, which we welcomed after the strains of the previous year. There would be moments when, watching Jesus sleeping, I would think of the future, wondering what it would hold for this little boy. I knew such hopes and yet, sometimes, such fears.

One day, our time of calm was suddenly shattered when a group of foreigners arrived. I was inside playing with Jesus when they entered our home and said that they had come to see my son. The men were beautifully dressed; without a doubt they were wealthy. In my confusion I rose, flustered by their sudden appearance and aware of our obvious poverty. Thoughts of the visit that we had received from the shepherds came into my mind. In my spirit I sensed that God was at work: this visit was somehow part of God's plan for his Son.

Quietly I set about providing my guests with food and drinks. When I turned back towards them, I was astonished by what I saw: these men of obvious status were kneeling on my rough floor, their heads touching the ground before them. Jesus was directly in front of them, standing uncharacteristically still, his eyes fixed on them.

'They know', I thought to myself. 'They know who he is.'

'We have gifts for your son,' one of them said to me as he rose. From their bags they drew out gold, frankincense and myrrh. What did they signify? I was to ponder on those gifts.

As I served the men, they told me their story. They were magi, wise men, from Babylon, who had been studying their ancient manuscripts as well as some of our Jewish manuscripts, which had remained in their land when our exiles had returned to Jerusalem. From these they had discovered that a newborn king would be born to the Jews, the King of all kings. They recognised that the time for his birth had come when a star of great brightness arose, and they had felt compelled to find the king and worship him.

They told me of the adventures of their journey, of their arrival in Jerusalem, their audience with King Herod and the agitation they saw in his face when they asked the whereabouts of this new king. Herod had consulted with the priests and teachers of religious law as to where the Messiah was expected to be born, and the eventual answer had been found within our scriptures: 'And you, O Bethlehem in the land of Judah, are not least among the ruling cities of Judah, for a ruler will come from you who will be the shepherd for my people Israel.'[25]

They had been looking in the wrong place. The king saw them privately, urging them to search for the child and to return to him with news of the boy so that he, too, could worship him. So they had hurried in the direction of Bethlehem, and that same star had glowed brightly, assuring them that they were soon to find the child, filling them with inexpressible joy.

As they spoke, my heart filled with excitement. Was my child to be recognized as the Chosen One so soon?

The men returned several times to spend time with Jesus, and my family was soon the talk of the town once again. On what was to be their final visit, though, the mood of the magi was very different. Urgently they spoke to me of a dream from God, warning them not to return to Herod. They were all sure of the warning and had determined to go back to their land by another route.

Joseph was greatly concerned when I told him of their dream. Indeed, he had been becoming increasingly nervous about the attention we were receiving from our neighbours and the possibility of one of Herod's men overhearing their chatter about this special baby. So when Joseph woke me one night, whispering that we were to leave immediately, for God had warned him in a dream to take us to safety in Egypt, I responded straight away. My heart beating fast, I quickly packed food and blankets, wrapping the gifts Jesus had received within them, while Joseph prepared our donkey. It was essential that we were away before dawn, before anyone saw us or questioned us, before anyone could see the direction in which we had left.

'What did God tell you in the dream?' I whispered to my husband as he fastened to the donkey the few belongings we were taking. Joseph took my hands in his. 'Herod is searching for Jesus. He plans to kill him.'

The life of my son was under threat. I moved in panic across to my sleeping child and scooped him into my arms, reassuring him as he stirred, singing his favourite song so quietly that only he could hear. We walked through the streets, Jesus held close to my heart. Joseph was looking anxiously around, no doubt concerned that the clopping of the donkey's hooves would wake people. Finally we left Bethlehem behind us. I mounted our donkey and Jesus slept as Joseph walked silently and swiftly beside us.

Terrible stories followed us to our new life in Egypt. Herod, in his rage at being outwitted by the magi, had ordered the death of every boy in Bethlehem under the age of two. While I thanked the Lord for our escape and marvelled at God's protection of his Son, I grieved deeply for those young boys. I grieved for my friends who had lost their treasured little ones while I still held mine.

Time passed and, although we grew accustomed to our life in Egypt, we longed for the time when God would bring us back to our own land and fulfil his promises regarding his Son. We rejoiced when news reached Egypt that Herod had died. God's word came to Joseph in a dream that it was now safe for us to return. At last our wait was over!

Initially we had planned to return to Judea but once again God spoke to Joseph, warning us of the threat that Herod's son, Archelaus, posed. So it was that we returned to my family's town of Nazareth, where my story had begun. With the lapse of time, the attitudes towards us there had softened and I was able to watch my son grow up in an atmosphere of acceptance. Although I thought so often about his early life, I said not a word.

Reflection and discussion

- Did any words or phrases stand out for you? Before further discussion, read the passage again in a different translation or paraphrase of the Bible.

- In the monologue, Mary is seen as enjoying a time of peace, which brought her restoration after the strain of the previous year. The word 'restore' has two meanings in Greek: to re-set what has been broken and to remove what is threatening. God is our restorer. He re-sets what is broken: 'Though you have made me see troubles, many and bitter, you will restore my life again; from the depths of the earth you will again bring me up' (Psalm 71:20, NIV). He also removes what is threatening: 'He makes me lie down in green pastures, he leads me beside quiet waters, he restores my soul' (Psalm 23:2–3, NIV 1984). Share times when God has restored you, either by re-setting what has been broken or by removing what is threatening.

- Do we, like Mary, oscillate between hopes and fears for ourselves and those we love when we think about the future? There are times when fear is appropriate because it enables us to take necessary action. However, fear can become crippling, affecting our ability to take action and even damaging our health. Give examples from your lives when you have known either a motivating fear or a crippling fear. How do you deal with fear? Many people in the Bible are told not to be afraid. David had the personal conviction that 'goodness and love will follow me all the days of my life, and I will dwell in the house of the Lord for ever' (Psalm 23:6, NIV).

- God brought the news of his Son's birth to the wealthy as well as the poor. Whatever our wealth or status, we all have a spiritual thirst, including the need for forgiveness and purpose. A wise teacher once described it thus: 'God... has planted eternity in the human heart' (Ecclesiastes 3:11). If time permits, read Matthew 19:16–26. Jesus said that it is harder for a camel to go through the eye of a needle than for a rich man to enter the kingdom of God. Why is this? Is it partly because of the humility required, the humility that the magi demonstrated when they knelt on a humble floor before a baby and worshipped him?

- What do you think is the significance of each of the gifts? Traditionally it is thought that gold represented Christ's kingship, frankincense signified the presence of God and myrrh indicated death and burial. One hymn speaks of the 'gold of obedience' and the 'incense of lowliness'.[26] Why do you think these expressions are used?

- The coming of the wise men, as they are traditionally called, is known as Epiphany. This event is remembered on 6 January, at the end of the traditional twelve days of Christmas. How could you celebrate this day with your family or in your own spiritual life? 'Epiphany' has come to mean a moment of great insight or revelation or an encounter with God. Encourage each other by sharing some of your epiphanies.

- We are always particularly affected by atrocities against children. What can we do to work for justice for children at local, national and international levels?

- There are many reasons why people become refugees, such as war, famine, threats to safety and religious persecution. Discuss practical ways to support displaced people who may now live in your community.

- Joseph, Mary and Jesus remained in Egypt until they received the go-ahead from God, through a dream, to return to Israel. Share your experiences of how God has led you to a new place or in a new direction.

- There are four instances of God leading through dreams in this episode (Matthew 2:12, 13, 19, 22). Has God spoken to you through dreams? If you are able, share these experiences.

Conclusion

Take time to pray through your findings. What might God be saying to you? Is anything particularly relevant to your life at the moment? Write down what you have learnt and refer back to it regularly in the days ahead so that it becomes part of your thinking, reacting and lifestyle.

Mary and the
twelve-year-old Jesus

Introduction

- Read Luke 2:41–52.
- Ask God to speak to you through this episode. You could use the words from Psalm 119:68: 'You are good, and the source of good; train me in your goodness' (*The Message*).
- Sit back, relax and close your eyes. Imagine the scene as someone reads out the monologue.

Monologue

The highlights of our quiet life in Nazareth were the three annual visits that we made to Jerusalem to celebrate the feast of Unleavened Bread, the feast of Weeks and the feast of Tabernacles. We took with us gifts according to the blessing we had received from the Lord that year. Jesus loved these occasions: he was always full of questions, hungry to learn. He loved, too, meeting up with family and friends.

When Jesus was twelve, we travelled up to Jerusalem to celebrate Passover, the feast of Unleavened Bread. It was a spring feast, the largest of our festivals, and the atmosphere was joyful as we remembered how God had passed over the home of every Israelite, protecting their firstborn, and how our people had packed unleavened bread for their journey out of Egypt.

Jesus loved these stories of our people's history; he loved to hear how a perfect lamb had been slaughtered for a feast and eaten along with bitter herbs and unleavened bread, while the blood of the lamb was placed over the doors as the sign for God to pass over that home. He loved the part of the story when our people dressed up before they ate the feast, ready to leave Egypt, sandals and cloaks on and walking sticks in their hands, showing their faith in the God who was about to act mightily on their behalf. Each year I saw his love for God growing and watched him develop in his understanding of our laws and traditions. So perhaps I should have known.

At the end of the celebrations, Joseph and I packed up and started to head back to Nazareth along with many friends and relatives. I had my hands full with the younger children. Jesus was nowhere to be seen but I assumed he was walking with the men at the back; at twelve he was practically an adult.

As evening approached, we found a place to settle for the night and I prepared food. There was still no sign of Jesus. Joseph had not seen him walking with the men; he had thought Jesus was at the front with us. I felt the first pangs of worry. Immediately, my husband set off to search the camp for Jesus.

Joseph was gone a long time. Pushing my thoughts to one side, I fed the other children and started to settle the youngest ones for the night. When he eventually returned, one look at his face told me that something was wrong.

'I've looked everywhere, spoken to our relatives, searched out all his friends, but no one has seen him. He hasn't been seen at all today. Mary, we've left him behind,' Joseph told me.

'As soon as it is daylight, we will return to Jerusalem. Your family has said that they will take the other children on with them tomorrow. We'll find Jesus and catch up with the others before they get to Nazareth. The three of us will be able to travel quickly without the young and old people,' he continued.

Joseph was trying so hard to be positive for my sake but I knew that anxious look in his eyes. I slept little that night. However much I told myself it had been reasonable to assume that Jesus was with the men, I fretted over my lack of action. I regretted that we had not checked who Jesus had planned to travel with before we set out, that we had not looked for him earlier. When had Jesus gone missing? Was he definitely still in the city? Where would we start looking for him among the crowds filling the streets of Jerusalem? I prayed feverishly for God's protection over his Son, prayed that we would find Jesus safe and well, and prayed for protection for us as we travelled without the safety of a group.

The next two days were dark and difficult. We went from one end of the city to the other, describing Jesus to all who would listen. So many young men fitted his description. We followed endless leads, but all to no avail. Exhaustion and desperation set in. I remembered those in Jerusalem who had wanted to kill Jesus when he was a young child and started to fear the worst.

On the third day of searching, we felt that there was nowhere else to look. Wearily we headed towards the temple itself to offer our prayers to God, to ask for mercy and help. As we approached, Joseph continued to describe our son to those leaving the temple. Then came the words we had been longing to hear: yes, there was a young man who met our description in the temple courts; he was sitting among the great rabbis of our land who had gathered for the Passover. The temple worshipper had gone nearer to listen to this young man and had been amazed at the depth of the questions that he asked and the answers that he gave. Quite a crowd had been gathering to listen to the debate.

A fresh surge of energy propelled us into the temple courts and suddenly we saw our son, just as we had been told, surrounded by teachers and onlookers. The fear and anxiety that I had been holding back came out in a torrent of accusation. Rushing up to Jesus, I burst out, 'My son, why have you done this to us? Your father and I have been frantic with worry.'

With concern for us in his eyes, he gave a reply that was to puzzle us for many days to come—words that, in the quiet moments, often returned to me. 'But why did you need to search for me? Didn't you know that I had to be in my Father's house?'

Gradually I came to the realisation. I had heard words from the angel Gabriel about my son: 'He will be great and be called the Son of the Most High.' We had fretted and searched; the temple of God, his dwelling place, had been the last place we had come to. As Jesus had said, we should have known that he would be in his Father's house.

Our return to Nazareth was accompanied by much celebration with family and friends. How they loved Jesus! In the years ahead, as I saw Jesus shoot up to adult height, I noticed how highly he was regarded by them all. He was wise in everything he said and did, and the blessing of God was upon him.

Reflection and discussion

■ Did any words or phrases stand out for you? Before further discussion, read the passage again in a different translation or paraphrase of the Bible.

- In Deuteronomy 16:16–17 we read of God's requirement that his people should celebrate the feast of Unleavened Bread, the feast of Weeks and the feast of Tabernacles. The Jewish calendar included many times of celebration, as does the Christian one. Celebration is part of God's plan for us in the rhythm of life. Why is celebration important? How does it help us? Advent, Christmas, Lent, Easter, the Ascension and Pentecost are all important in the Christian calendar. Which do you celebrate and how? Share ideas of ways in which you can start to celebrate the other festivals. Remember that celebration can be outward (with large groups, such as your church community, or with smaller groups, such as friends or relatives) or inward (celebration in solitude, such as following an Advent or Lent course).

- When attending the Passover feast, the people were required to bring a gift in proportion to the way the Lord had blessed them over the previous year. Giving according to the blessing we have received is a principle that appears in the Old and New Testament. Jesus said, 'Give as freely as you have received' (Matthew 10:8). We are encouraged to see all that we have—materially, socially and spiritually—as blessings from God. The Bible promises that God will provide for the generous giver. Read the following verses and then share experiences that reveal the truth of these promises: 'Give generously to the poor, not grudgingly, for the Lord your God will bless you in everything you do' (Deuteronomy 15:10). 'You must each decide in your heart how much to give. And don't give reluctantly or in response to pressure. "For God loves a person who gives cheerfully." And God will generously provide all you need. Then you will always have everything you need and plenty left over to share with others' (2 Corinthians 9:7–8).

■ Holy Week, the name the church gives to the last week of Jesus' life, also took place during the Passover festival. The Passover celebration took on new meaning when Jesus, the Lamb of God, used bread and wine during the last supper with his disciples to symbolise his body and blood, which were to be given for us. Jesus said, 'Do this in remembrance of me' (Luke 22:19, NIV). For this reason we solemnly celebrate Communion. Share how this service is meaningful for you or tell of a specific Communion service that was of significance to you.

■ In the monologue, Mary faces guilt and self-accusation. It was natural for Mary and Joseph to assume that Jesus was with the other parent, as it was customary for women and children to travel at the front and men at the back. At the age of twelve, Jesus could have been with either group. Like Mary, we can blame ourselves, sometimes irrationally, for outcomes in our lives. Our inner dialogue can become full of self-accusation: 'I should have done this', 'I shouldn't have done that', or 'If only I had…' God provides both forgiveness from true guilt and freedom from false guilt. How can we know the difference between true and false guilt? How can we move into a deeper experience of freedom from false guilt?

■ It can be easy to overlook the fact that Jesus was a Jewish boy, learning the stories, laws and traditions of his people. He 'grew in wisdom' as he studied the scriptures and experienced life, living in close relationship with God at all times (Luke 2:52). In this episode we saw Jesus listening to and questioning the religious teachers, developing insight. Share ideas about how we can grow in wisdom, for we are promised wisdom if we ask God for it: 'If you need wisdom, ask our generous God, and he will give it to you' (James 1:5).

■ When we ask God for character attributes, such as wisdom and the fruit of the Spirit (Galatians 5:22–23), God will provide us with situations in which we can develop the quality requested. For example, to learn patience we will meet with situations in which we have to persevere and hence acquire patience. Share your experiences of such situations.

■ In this episode, the twelve-year-old Jesus had the opportunity to listen, ask questions and give answers that amazed everyone who heard because of the depth of his understanding. It is important that we allow young people to ask their questions freely and that we listen to their understanding and insights. How can we create an atmosphere that encourages this freedom in our families, churches and communities?

■ When we are under pressure or very tired, we can often react in ways that we later regret. Mary's reaction when she saw Jesus was very human. We know that Jesus never sinned and yet, as a result of his action, his parents suffered greatly. How do you understand this apparent conflict?

■ Jesus was seeing the situation from a different perspective. Even the Lord's parents had to learn to trust their adolescent child and see life from his perspective. Misunderstandings with family members, friends and colleagues, as well as within the Christian community, often result from a difference of perspective. Share your experiences of such misunderstandings and your strategies to avoid or overcome them.

■ What have you learnt of Jesus, the Son of God, from this study?

Conclusion

Take time to pray through your findings. What might God be saying to you? Is anything particularly relevant to your life at the moment? Write down what you have learnt and refer back to it regularly in the days ahead so that it becomes part of your thinking, reacting and lifestyle.

Jesus and Mary
at the wedding in Cana

Introduction

- Read John 2:1–12.

- Ask God to speak to you through this episode. You could use the words from Psalm 119:64: 'Your love, God, fills the earth! Train me to live by your counsel' (THE MESSAGE).

- Sit back, relax and close your eyes. Imagine the scene as someone reads out the monologue.

Monologue

It was wonderful to be at our friends' wedding celebration in the company of my son—a rare treat now. I was taking the opportunity to observe him, which had been my habit ever since his birth. He was relaxed, laughing and talking with his friends. I say 'friends' but his relationship with them was more than one of friendship: I heard them call him 'Rabbi' or 'Teacher'. Oh, the time had been so long in coming, these birthpangs of recognition! I had waited and watched, watched and waited as the years went by. I had expected him to make clear who he was, the Son of the Most High, so much earlier, especially after the episode in the Jerusalem temple when he was only twelve. Ever since then, I had anticipated something happening, although I could never quite formulate in my own mind what this something would be... perhaps the emergence of my son as a great Jewish leader.

Jesus had supported our family, taking over from Joseph as the carpenter, until the other boys were old enough to take his place, and then he had spent more time with his cousin John and more time alone. Once he returned from a 40-day fast in the wilderness, exhausted and haggard, as if he carried the weight of the world on his shoulders. And still I waited, treasuring in my heart the promises that the angel had spoken some 30 years ago: 'He will be holy, the Son of God, the Most High. He will have an everlasting kingdom.'

Perhaps it was this lifetime habit of watching and listening that made me realise there was a problem at the wedding. I sensed the shuffling and muttering among the servants and, when the opportunity came, I asked one what was wrong, only to discover that the wine was running out. What humiliation for my friends! I went over to Jesus, for although there had never been a public demonstration of his power, I knew who he truly was and had no doubt that he could help to prevent this embarrassment.

'They have no more wine,' I whispered.

He looked at me with his kindly, tender eyes. 'Dear mother, that's not our problem. My time has not yet come.'

They were not words of criticism but were enough of a rebuke for me to understand that my son was going to make his decisions in his own time and in his own way. Letting go of him, my firstborn, had always been hard, as I had more than the usual hopes for him, to say the least…

Still, as I returned to my seat, I said quietly to the panic-stricken servants, 'Do whatever my son tells you.'

When I next looked at Jesus, there was a sparkle in his eye, as if he was about to enjoy himself enormously. I sat back and watched. Jesus approached the servants and asked them to fill to the brim with water the six large ceremonial jars used for washing. The servants seemed confused, for the ceremonial washing was long past. However, an order was an order, so they went ahead. I could see Jesus' lips moving and then one of the servants putting some of the water into wine cups and walking with trepidation to the Master of Ceremonies. He handed over the cup to him and then made a hasty retreat as the Master took his first mouthful. The expression on the Master's face was a picture: he gazed into the wine cup and slowly took another sip. Looking for the nearest servant, he demanded that the bridegroom be brought to him. The servants looked frightened; were they to lose their jobs for serving water instead of wine?

The bridegroom hurried over. 'You've served your wine in the wrong order,' the Master of Ceremonies said. 'Most people serve the best wine first and then serve the wine of lesser quality when everyone has had plenty to drink and won't know the difference. But this is the best wine I've ever tasted!'

I will never forget the look of relief on the faces of the servants and the amazement in the eyes of my son's friends. It was at that moment that they truly believed in him with heartfelt conviction. I caught my son's gaze and the joy that I saw there will stay with me for the rest of my life.

Reflection and discussion

- Did any words or phrases stand out to you? Before further discussion, read the passage again in a different translation or paraphrase of the Bible.

- Mary had to 'let go' of Jesus. Letting go of situations and people can be difficult. It is a step of faith to trust difficult situations and those we love to God. It is easy to let our concern become interference. Share situations where you have struggled and learnt to let go. What has been the outcome? Share situations where you still need to learn this, and support one another in what you share.

■ This episode in the life of Jesus shows him celebrating and bringing joy, as do many others in the Gospels. So often, our lives can lose this element of celebration and joy. Why? How can it be recreated, both in our personal lives and as a group of believers?

■ New wine is a symbol for the coming of the kingdom of God. Read Luke 5:33–39. What do the words of Jesus in this encounter and in the parables teach us? In what ways do we try to put new wine into old wineskins?

■ Wine was also significant at the last supper, representing the blood of Christ. Read Luke 22:14–20. Jesus says that he will not drink wine again until the kingdom of God comes. Ponder on the fact that the wine speaks both of joy and death, celebration and sacrifice.

■ We are told that the disciples believed in Jesus after seeing this miracle. Can you recall significant moments in your life when your faith was taken to new limits by seeing God at work in your life or by seeing or reading of God working in the lives of others? Share these moments.

■ How has looking at these passages enabled you to 'know' Jesus, the Son of God, more? Jesus is the 'Word become flesh' (John 1:14, NIV) and, in 'knowing' him, we know God the Father, for Jesus 'radiates God's own glory and expresses the very character of God' (Hebrews 1:3).

Conclusion

Take time to pray through your findings. What might God be saying to you? Is anything particularly relevant to your life at the moment? Write down what you have learnt and refer back to it regularly in the days ahead so that it becomes part of your thinking, reacting and lifestyle.

Jesus and
the Samaritan woman

Introduction

- Read John 4:4–30, 39–42.

- Ask God to speak to you through this episode. You could use
  the words from Psalm 119:174: 'O Lord, I have longed for
  your rescue, and your instructions are my delight.'

- Sit back, relax and close your eyes. Imagine the scene as
  someone reads out the monologue.

Monologue

I was on my way to get water when I first saw him. He looked
exhausted and was sitting leaning against the well. So I
wasn't the only one to brave the midday sun. For me, it was
the way to avoid the looks and gossip of the other women
of my village; I preferred to lessen their opportunity to make
digs at me. You see, I had a past. It wasn't that I was afraid
of them; I always had an answer for anyone. I had built a wall
of protection around myself over the years; it was a wall of
sharp answers and witty retorts, a wall that I thought was
impenetrable.

As I reached the well, he looked up and said, 'Please give
me a drink.'

That caught me off guard.

'What are you doing asking me for a drink? You're a Jew,
and I'm a Samaritan—and a woman at that, in case you hadn't

noticed. The likes of you have nothing to do with the likes of me,' was my pointed reply.

His next words were gentle, wistful even. 'If only you knew the gift God has for you, and who it is speaking with you, you would ask me for living water.'

'Oh yes? And how, may I ask, are you going to get this living water? You don't have a rope or a bucket! This well is deep. Besides, are you suggesting any well could be better than the one given by our ancestor, Jacob? Do you realise this well in Sychar was the one he gave to his son, Joseph, for his family and animals to use?'

I detected a slight glint of amusement in his eyes as I said this—not exactly the response I had expected.

His reply seemed to ignore the antagonism in my words.

'Anyone drinking the water from this well will soon be thirsty again. But those who drink the water that I give will find that they will never thirst again; it will bubble up from inside like a fresh stream, giving them eternal life.'

With a hint of sarcasm, but thinking it wise to humour this man, I quickly replied, 'Please, sir, give me this water. Then I won't have to do this chore every day.'

'First get your husband, then I can give it to you both,' he said.

'Ah! Impossible. I don't have a husband!' I said triumphantly.

'True,' he replied, 'You don't have a husband. You've had five, and the man you live with now is not your husband. You certainly spoke the truth.'

Momentarily I was lost for words. Who was this man? Still, he was not going to get the better of me. I was challenge enough for any man!

'I see you are a prophet, so can you answer me this? Why can Jews and Samaritans not even agree about where we should worship? You Jews say Jerusalem and we say Mount Gerazim, which is where our ancestors worshipped.'

I wished to stir up argument, to take the conversation away from my life.

It was his reply that completely undid me and broke down that long erected wall, for he called me 'dear woman'. I had only heard such words from men who wanted something. I saw gentleness and sincerity in his eyes.

'Dear woman, believe me when I say that a time is coming when it will not matter where God is worshipped. You Samaritans do not know the God you long to worship, but we Jews *do*, for salvation is coming through the Jews to all people. The time is coming—in fact, it is here *now*—when all true worshippers will worship God in Spirit and in truth. For God is spirit and he is searching for those who will worship him, worship him in spirit and truth.'

This is what I wanted: to know God, to worship God. A deep emptiness within me longed for a relationship with God. There was so much that I didn't understand; I was struggling to grasp what he meant. Now my reply was hungry, open.

'I know that the Messiah will come, the Christ; when he comes, all these things will become clear.'

'I am he.'

As I stood gazing at him in wonder, I became aware that now we were surrounded by men carrying food. Their faces said it all—full of the rejection I was used to experiencing. But not him: he had not rejected me. I left my jar, turned and ran into the village, calling people to come and meet the man who knew all about me before I'd said a word.

'Could he be the Chosen One, the Messiah?'

They listened to *me* and they came!

We persuaded Jesus and his friends to stay for two days.

Those two days transformed my life and the lives of many in my village. For we believed that Jesus was the Saviour of the world!

Reflection and discussion

- Did any phrase or thought stand out for you? Before further discussion, read the passage again in a different translation or paraphrase of the Bible.

- Dealing with abrasive people can be a challenge. Read Matthew 7:1–5. Jesus warns us not to judge others. We might never know what has brought people to where they are, what has caused their aggressive attitudes. What can we learn from the way Jesus conversed with this woman? Share experiences of engaging with abrasive people and of breaking down barriers.

- The disciples were shocked to find Jesus talking to a woman. Perhaps their inability to challenge Jesus gives an indication of their awareness of their prejudice. Are there subtle ways in which we are not inclusive? How can we be more inclusive, both as individuals and as groups?

- What does it mean to worship God in spirit and in truth?

- Jesus was on his way back to Galilee and was passing through Samaria. In response to the Samaritans' request, he stayed two days. Are we willing to change our agenda if appropriate, or are we too driven? Share experiences.

- The woman went on a journey of faith, from belief that Jesus was a prophet to believing that he was the Messiah. Encourage one or two group members to describe their faith journey. Putting our spiritual story into spoken and/

or written words can prepare us for opportunities to speak about our faith. Try doing this in the week ahead.

■ Living water is one of the pictures of the Holy Spirit. The Holy Spirit is like a spring bubbling within us. We are instructed to continue being 'filled with the Spirit' (Ephesians 5:18, NIV). Share ways in which we can do this, so that we do not 'dry up'.

■ What have you learnt of God the Father, God the Son and God the Holy Spirit from this study? How does this enable you to know him more?

Conclusion

Take time to pray through your findings. What might God be saying to you? Is anything particularly relevant to your life at the moment? Write down what you have learnt and refer back to it regularly in the days ahead so that it becomes part of your thinking, reacting and lifestyle.

Jesus and Simon's mother-in-law

Introduction

- Read Luke 4:31–44; Mark 1:35–39; John 1:29–30, 35–42 and Mark 1:16–18. Some of these passages could be read before the monologue and some of them afterwards.

- Ask God to speak to you through this episode. You could use the words from Psalm 119:34: 'Give me understanding and I will obey your instructions; I will put them into practice with all my heart.'

- Sit back, relax and close your eyes. Imagine the scene as someone reads the monologue.

Monologue

Jesus had been with us for quite a few weeks by then, that memorable sabbath day. I had not known what to make of it all initially, or what to make of *him*, this man who had entered our lives and was turning them upside down. Indeed, his teaching in the synagogue each week had turned the whole of Capernaum upside down.

Although I had misgivings because of the disruption to my family, I found myself looking forward to the sabbath, to the next time I would hear Jesus speak. He was like no other rabbi I had heard, for he spoke with authority—his own authority. After Jesus had finished teaching, he would come to our house, Simon's house, with his friends. My daughter and I would feed them while conversation and laughter flowed.

We valued these moments, my daughter and I, for we knew that Jesus and his disciples would not be in Capernaum for ever. Once more we would be on our own, missing Simon, missing Jesus, managing as best we could.

That day was different, though. I had woken with a fever. Struggling off my bed, I fell to the floor, dizzy and hot. My daughter insisted that I lie down, instructing me to rest while she took the family to the synagogue. Disappointment gripped me: this could be the last sabbath they were here, my last opportunity to hear Jesus.

Then worry took the place of disappointment. How was my daughter going to manage to feed all the men alone, without me there in the background, helping? Perhaps some of the women who travelled with Jesus would help, but I knew the routine. I was indispensable, wasn't I?

The fever increased: one moment my body was burning and the next incredibly cold. Now fear knocked at the door: was I walking through the valley of the shadow of death? My neck was stiff, my headache was raging and my eyes were tender and intolerant to light. Even shutting my eyes did not create enough darkness.

I don't know whether I was dreaming or awake but the start of it all came back to me with intense clarity—Simon coming home brimming with excitement, enthusiasm shining through every word that he spoke to his wife. I had sat quietly in the corner, cuddling one of the grandchildren, a coldness gripping my heart. Where was this going to lead?

It had begun with Andrew, really—Simon's brother. They are—or should I say, they were—fishing partners. Andrew is quieter and more reflective than Simon, thinks before he speaks and acts, but he had become passionate about hearing the teacher, John. After the fish were caught and the nets were washed, Andrew would go off in search of him. Then he became John's disciple and began spending more time away from the fishing. Andrew told Simon that he was waiting for something more to happen, something more than John's call to repentance, for John was preparing the way for the Lord's coming.

Then one day Andrew had seen a man approach John— apparently his cousin, Jesus. John turned to those around him and said, 'Look, here is the Lamb of God, who takes away the sins of the world. He is the one I was talking about.'

The next day, Andrew was once again with John when the cousin came by. John said, 'Look, the Lamb of God.' Andrew and another disciple followed Jesus. Everything had become crystal clear in Andrew's mind: *this* was the man. Jesus turned round and asked them what they wanted.

'Where are you staying?' Andrew had asked.

'Come and see,' Jesus replied.

Apparently Andrew spent the whole day with Jesus. Simon was used to his brother spending time with John, returning pensive and working quietly through the night. But this was different—as are all the days when Jesus breaks through into someone's life. Andrew rushed up to Simon and said, 'Come with me. We have found the Messiah. Come and see.'

The Messiah, the long-awaited one, here in our generation after years of silence and oppression? Could it be? I would have stayed rooted to the spot, disbelieving, even cynical. But Peter was impulsive, open-hearted, trusting, keen to be in on the action and never one to miss excitement. So he went, and those steps to Jesus changed our lives, for they changed Simon, even his name. When Jesus met Simon, he said, 'Your name is Simon, son of John, but you will be called Cephas or Peter, the rock.'

That is why Simon had returned home so animated and why we started to call him Simon-Peter.

It wasn't long before we started to realise the implications of this meeting. One day, Simon-Peter returned from work to say that he and Andrew had been fishing when Jesus had called to them, 'Follow me and I will show you how to fish for people.' They had left their nets and followed him.

And that is how our lives came to be changed—my daughter's, the children's and mine. We celebrated with joy when Jesus and his followers were here. When they were gone, my daughter maintained a determined trust in her husband, in his calling to be with Jesus. She was proud, but she was lonely too. I could see it in her eyes and she became so quiet. How she missed his talk and larger-than-life personality. So, as I said, we managed as best we could and I kept my mouth shut about my qualms.

These musings tumbled around in my aching head, becoming distorted and muddled as the fever rose.

I must have been asleep when they returned from the synagogue. I remember the sudden noise and my desire for silence. Anxious voices surrounded me as they begged Jesus to help me. I was aware of a sudden hush and his presence. I could not open my eyes, but I knew that he was there, beside me. Then his words broke the silence: 'Leave her.'

I felt his hand on mine—cool, refreshing—and he drew me up. Immediately any sign of fever and weakness left me. Laughter and joy filled the room. I looked over at my daughter and saw tears of relief in her eyes. I suggested that we got food for everyone and she responded with a smile of agreement.

What a day! As we ate, I heard about what had happened in the synagogue, how a man with a demon had called out to

Jesus, 'Why are you interfering with us, Jesus of Nazareth?' Jesus had cast the evil spirit out of the man, much to the amazement of everyone present.

Then my healing! By evening, people were flocking to our house and bringing with them those who were sick or possessed. Jesus released them from their suffering. That day my doubts left me, for as the demons yelled, 'You are the Son of God!' my heart echoed, 'Yes, you are the Messiah.'

The next day I rose early, wanting to speak to Jesus, but he was not there. As time went on, I became concerned and went with Simon-Peter and the others to look for him. At last, on the outskirts of the village, we saw Jesus walking towards us. Simon-Peter told Jesus that everyone was searching for him. From out of nowhere a crowd started to gather, pressing Jesus to stay, but Jesus replied that he and the disciples must go on to other towns. So they left Capernaum.

My daughter and I... well, we managed as best we could.

Reflection and discussion

■ Did any words or phrases stand out for you? Before further discussion, read some or all of the passages again in a different translation or paraphrase of the Bible.

■ In this monologue, we imagined Simon-Peter's mother-in-law experiencing different emotions as she became more and more unwell.

  – She felt great disappointment at not being able to attend the synagogue. Recall events that you have missed or disappointments that you have experienced, be they minor or major, remembering that what seems like a minor disappointment may actually signify a deeper hurt. Share these experiences if you are able. How can we allow God's grace into such situations?

– She became anxious as the fever increased. Her anxiety focused on how her daughter would manage to feed such a crowd without her help. It is easy to feel that we are indispensable and it can be hard to discover that we are not. Share your experiences of this. Just as we can trust God to provide for us, we can also trust him to provide for those we love.

– Finally, she feared that her illness might result in death. It is easy for our thoughts to run away with us, to allow our thinking to become negative and to fear the worst. In 2 Corinthians 10:5 we read, 'We take captive every thought to make it obedient to Christ' (NIV). We are instructed in Romans 12:2 to 'let God transform you into a new person by changing the way you think.' How can we take steps to allow God to transform our thinking patterns? How can we take thoughts captive?

■ Simon's mother-in-law played a supportive background role. Perhaps you do the same, or perhaps you have others who take a supportive position, enabling you to fulfil your role. Share ways in which you enable others or are enabled by others. In what ways can taking a supportive role be difficult? Are there ways in which you could show gratitude to those who have supported you?

■ In this monologue we see that there is a cost for the whole family when Simon-Peter follows Jesus. What do you know of this in your family? Do you know families who are paying a price for their commitment to Christ, for whom you could pray?

■ Simon-Peter's mother-in-law received healing from Jesus and then was able to wait on her guests. Being blessed by Christ led to her blessing others, which resulted in her being further blessed. Jesus said, 'Give, and you will receive. Your gift will return to you in full—pressed down, shaken together to make room for more, running over, and poured into your lap' (Luke 6:38). We are promised, 'Those who refresh others will themselves be refreshed' (Proverbs 11:25). How have you seen this principle at work in your life? Share your thoughts.

■ In this episode we see an outpouring of God's grace on Capernaum. Jesus' authority is shown in his teaching, healing and power over evil spirits as he brings restoration to many people. Although the people came to look for him the next day, pressing him to stay, Jesus was not distracted from his goal: 'I must proclaim the good news of the kingdom of God to the other towns also, because that is why I was sent' (Luke 4:43, NIV). Prayerfully setting goals, both short-term and long-term, can help us to keep focused, protect us from distractions and give us purpose. We need great sensitivity to the Spirit of God to know when to say 'yes' and when to say 'no' to seemingly worthy distractions. Do you prayerfully set goals? Has it been helpful? Have you had occasions when, like Jesus at the end of this episode, you have had to walk away from other people's demands because you have known that you have had other priorities? This can be very difficult. Share your experiences.

■ 'At daybreak, Jesus went out to a solitary place' (Luke 4:42, NIV). Jesus sought quietness to spend time with God. This gave him the wisdom and insight to set priorities within his ministry, as well as giving him strength for what lay ahead. Share how you find time to spend with God and the impact this has on your daily life.

■ What does this episode reveal about Jesus that helps us to know and enjoy him more?

Conclusion

Take time to pray through your findings. What might God be saying to you? Is anything particularly relevant to your life at the moment? Write down what you have learnt and refer back to it regularly in the days ahead so that it becomes part of your thinking, reacting and lifestyle.

Jesus and the prostitute

Introduction

- Read Luke 5:27–32 and 7:36–50.

- Ask God to speak to you through this episode. You could use the words from Psalm 119:73: 'With your very own hands you formed me; now breathe your wisdom over me so I can understand you' (THE MESSAGE).

- Sit back, relax and close your eyes. Imagine the scene as someone reads out the monologue.

Monologue

I had met Jesus at Levi's house. We prostitutes often socialised with the tax-collectors. They were unpopular because they worked for the Romans and because they often cheated to improve their standard of living. This gave them plenty of money to pay for our services. The prostitutes and tax collectors were the scum of Jewish society, and that bound us together.

But Levi had changed: he had given up his lucrative job to follow the prophet, Jesus. He had invited us all to a banquet so that we too could meet Jesus. I was cynical about men: you are when you have been in my trade for a while. Jesus, however, was different. He was good and pure; he spoke to us rather than at us. He treated us with respect. He spoke of God's great love for us, of forgiveness and of the possibility of new life. He told us stories and, if you listened carefully, you could work out what he was getting at. He said that only the sick needed doctors.

I was fascinated. I was also distraught, for the longer he spoke, the more I could see the darkness in my life. I had become an empty shell as each encounter with a man chipped off another fragment of my soul. Jesus stressed that he had come to call those who knew they were sinners; he had come to show them that a righteous life was possible. I looked across at Levi. Wasn't he living proof that this was true?

In my heart I said, 'Me, too, Jesus. I need God's forgiveness. I want to live a different life.' It was as though a huge burden rolled off my back and a glorious love, a pure light, coursed through my body. A new hope filled my being.

It wasn't easy, though. How was I to earn my bread? I wavered between an overwhelming joy and moments of doubt and panic. But then I would remember Jesus, and the release and peace I had known that night. My love for him grew—a pure, untainted love. I longed to see him again.

Soon my opportunity came. I heard that Jesus was eating at the home of one of the Pharisees. In my possession I had a beautiful alabaster jar of expensive perfume, one of the luxuries acquired through my trade. I knew I would have to act quickly, for I would be unwelcome in such a home and would in all likelihood be removed. But I had to thank Jesus for what he had done for me that other night. Creeping in, I saw Jesus reclining at the table. From where I stood, I could approach him from behind. I moved forwards slowly and silently, becoming aware that there was tension in the air; it was so different from the mood of celebration that we had known in Levi's home.

As I knelt at Jesus' feet, a gasp of horror escaped my lips.

His feet were filthy. My Jesus had not been welcomed into this house; he had not been treated with respect, as an equal. The tears started to roll down my face. Why had they treated him in this way? Oh, the tears—I could not stop the flow: tears for him, tears of sorrow for my wasted years, empowering tears that were to wash away the past and enable me to start afresh. I noticed that my tears were falling on his feet, washing them. Tenderly I dried his feet with my hair and poured my perfume on them. The aroma rose and filled the room. I kissed his feet over and over again with pure kisses.

The conversation had stopped and I heard one of the Pharisees muttering to himself, 'If Jesus was a prophet, he would not have allowed this, for he would have known that this woman is immoral.' Jesus appeared to change the subject, saying to him, 'Simon, I want to tell you a story.'

'Go ahead,' said Simon.

I strained to listen, continuing to pour perfume on the feet of Jesus, and to kiss them.

'A man loaned money to two people—500 pieces of silver to one and 50 pieces to the other. Neither could repay him so he let them both off their debt. Who will love him the most?'

'The one let off the larger debt,' Simon replied.

'That's right,' said Jesus. 'Look at this woman. You did not extend me the courtesy of washing the dust from my feet, but she has washed them with tears; you did not offer me the kiss of greeting, but she has not stopped kissing my feet; you did not anoint my head with olive oil, yet she has anointed my feet with a rare perfume. She has been forgiven for her many sins and so she loves much. One who has been forgiven little loves little.'

Then Jesus turned round and looked me in the eyes. There was such a welcome there. 'Your sins are forgiven,' he said.

How I had needed to hear these words directed at *me*! Yet only God could forgive sins. Who was this man who forgave sins? I heard the men at the table asking the same question, but their words were harsh, accusing.

Still looking at me, Jesus said, 'Your faith has saved you. Go in peace.'

Reflection and discussion

■ Did any words or phrases stand out for you? Before further discussion, read the passage again in a different translation or paraphrase of the Bible.

■ Often, Jesus could be found sharing meals. His emphasis was on relationships and community rather than on structure and institutions. How can we share meals both within our homes and as larger groups, to build community and introduce others to Jesus? Share your experiences.

■ In the monologue, the woman wavered between faith and doubt. If we are honest, this is often our experience. What doubts do you face? Doubts can be viewed positively in that they force us to think through issues and hence to grow in our faith. Some of our questions may never be answered, and the acceptance of this fact can lead us to greater humility and trust in God. Share ways in which you deal with doubts.

■ Our love both for God and for others stems from God's love for us. Take time to meditate on 1 John 4:7–17 in the days ahead. God has many ways of showing us his love. We may experience God's love in our emotions, as the woman did in this monologue. However, God may be demonstrating his love to us in more subtle ways that we can easily miss if we are not attentive. It is said that

God 'whispers'. Brainstorm ways in which God shows his love—for example, in the meeting of a need at just the right moment or in the beauty of creation.

■ This episode tells of a woman's restoration. Jesus is our Redeemer. To 'redeem' means to pay the price required in order to buy something back that was already yours. Jesus has paid the price through his death to 'buy us back', in order to redeem our lives and to renew us. An Old Testament promise reads, 'I will repay you for the years the locusts have eaten' (Joel 2:25, NIV). We do not know what happened next to this woman. It is quite possible that she became one of the women who travelled with Jesus. We can only imagine. If appropriate, share times when God has restored you or brought good from what had seemed like wasted time.

■ In a society where 'anything goes', it is easy to lose a sense of the gravity of sin. Learning to live in ongoing repentance is an important part of our spiritual journey, so that we can experience the blessing of 'going in peace' and know freedom from guilt. What can we do to live in ongoing repentance? What are the advantages of confessing sin to one another? 'Confess your sins to each other and pray for each other so that you may be healed' (James 5:16).

■ Jesus claims in Luke 5:32, 'I have come to call... those who know they are sinners and need to repent.' In Luke 7:48, he goes further in saying to the woman, 'Your sins are forgiven.' This was a claim to be God, for only God can forgive sins.

■ What have you discovered about Jesus in these passages that will enable you to know him better and love him more?

Conclusion

Take time to pray through your findings. What might God be saying to you? Is anything particularly relevant to your life at the moment? Write down what you have learnt and refer back to it regularly in the days ahead so that it becomes part of your thinking, reacting and lifestyle.

Jesus and the widow of Nain

This and the following study both show Jesus putting the needs of women above rules and regulations. They could be covered in one session, depending on the time available. If so, the conclusion could be left until the end of the second study.

Introduction

- Read Luke 7:11–17.

- Ask God to speak to you through this episode. You could use the words from Psalm 119:173: 'Stand ready to help me because I have chosen to follow your will' (LB).

- Sit back, relax and close your eyes. Imagine the scene as someone reads out the monologue.

Monologue

I was numb with pain. It seemed unreal. I was walking with my family and neighbours behind my beloved only son's slender, still frame, carried on a stretcher. Only days ago he had been full of vitality, and suddenly illness had struck him—fever and then death. How could I have suffered a double blow in so short a time? Months ago we had mourned as we buried the body of my husband. Joshua had been my reason for carrying on, my hope for the future. He would work for us and provide for us. God had seemed close to me then in my grief; he was my comfort and strength. But now he seemed distant, even absent. How was I to bear it? How was I to survive?

As we walked through the streets of Nain, I was aware that Jesus, the prophet, had joined the procession with his companions. He moved forward until he was standing right next to me. My eyes met his and what I saw astonished me. I expected to see sympathy, but I found so much more— compassion and grief. Yes, grief. It was as though he was suffering the loss with me. 'Don't cry,' he said as he stepped forward, level with my boy.

Some people glared at him; this intrusion was unwelcome. Calmly he did the unthinkable: he stretched out his hand and touched the dead body of my child. Astonished eyes focused on this man. What was going on? Jesus kept his eyes on Joshua's face.

'He's stirring,' he said.

How could he be? My vision blurred with tears, I looked from Jesus to my son's face. Was I imagining it or was colour returning to Joshua's cheeks? Then the impossible happened. He opened his eyes and smiled the most heart-warming smile at me.

'Young man, get up,' Jesus instructed. The crowd gasped as Joshua sat up, slowly swung his legs over the side of the stretcher and stepped down.

What a moment it was as he fell into my arms! I wanted to hold him for ever. Shouts of amazement filled the air and mingled with our laughter. We found ourselves encircled by relatives and friends. Their cries of mourning were replaced with joyful singing and dancing. How we celebrated!

Reflection and discussion

- Did any words or phrases stand out for you? Before further discussion, read the passage again in a different translation or paraphrase of the Bible.

- Jesus broke with convention when he touched the dead body of the boy, for anyone who touched a corpse became ceremonially unclean (Numbers 19:11). Can you think of any times when you have broken with convention to follow him?

- ■ The death of a child is always a tragedy. Spend a moment in silent prayer, bringing before God the families of any you know who have lost a child and have to live with this pain throughout their lives.

- ■ Having an understanding of the progression of grief can help us in our own losses and in getting alongside others who have suffered loss. The stages of grief are denial, anger, depression and acceptance. These stages often overlap and a stage can be revisited or triggered by other events or memories. This is a normal part of the grieving process.

- ■ As in the monologue, sometimes God can feel very near when we are grieving, so that, in spite of our suffering, we know a deep peace. But it is also possible to feel that God is far away, particularly when we are depressed. If you feel able, share your experiences.

- ■ In this passage the Lord Jesus has a heart 'overflowing with compassion', revealing the heart of God the Father. Allow yourself to take this on board, particularly if you have a tendency to see God as stern, demanding or distant. Ask that God will 'grow' compassion in you through the work of the Holy Spirit.

Conclusion

Take time to pray through your findings. What might God be saying to you? Is anything particularly relevant to your life at the moment? Write down what you have learnt and refer back to it regularly in the days ahead so that it becomes part of your thinking, reacting and lifestyle.

Jesus and
the crippled woman

Introduction

- Read Luke 13:10–16.

- Ask God to speak to you through this episode. You could use the words from Psalm 119:77: 'Let your compassion come to me that I may live, for your law is my delight' (NIV).

- Sit back, relax and close your eyes. Imagine the scene as someone reads out the monologue.

Monologue

I had gone to the synagogue as was my custom, looking forward to hearing the prophet, Jesus, speak. I had heard so much about him. But I could not look up at him, for I had been crippled for 18 years, bent double. It was so long since I had followed the path of a bird in the sky or seen a smile break across a face. However, I had become an expert at under-standing a person's character by listening to the voice. Oh, voices tell us so much if we know how to listen. I knew by *his* voice that he was kind, holy, joyful, authoritative, determined and courageous. Lost in my thoughts and unable to see what was going on, I felt a hand push my back.

'It's you,' someone said. 'He's calling for you.'

Confused, I stumbled forwards in the direction of his voice, seeing feet part to allow me through. I was used to seeing feet instead of faces. You can tell a lot by someone's feet, too! A silence descended. I could sense that Jesus was looking at me. I longed to meet his gaze.

'Woman, you are set free from this infirmity.' His voice was tender.

I felt his touch on my back. Immediately a pulsing ran down me and I found myself straightening, stretching. I could see the people around me! I could look up at his face and I could see that I had understood his character correctly. Words of praise to God flowed from my mouth.

Then another voice broke in: 'There are six days to come for healing. Do not come to be healed on the sabbath.'

There was strong indignation in the voice of the synagogue ruler as he gave the instruction to all who had witnessed my healing. But I had not come to the synagogue asking for healing. I had come to listen. It was Jesus who had seen my suffering and had pity on me.

He had a stern answer for those clustering around the synagogue ruler. 'You hypocrites! You don't consider it work when you look after your animals on the sabbath. You untie them and meet their needs by leading them to water. So should not this woman who has been bound by Satan for 18 years not have her need met on the sabbath?'

I was set free! Standing tall and straight, I looked into the faces of my neighbours, saw their amazed expressions and enjoyed the warmth of their smiles. As we left the synagogue, I gazed with joy up at the sky and followed the path of a sparrow as it darted between the housetops. My delight in these simple pleasures has remained with me to this day.

Reflection and discussion

- Did any words or phrases stand out for you? Before further discussion, read the passage again in a different translation or paraphrase of the Bible.

- This is an account in which Jesus initiates the encounter. Sometimes he acted in response to the faith of the person needing healing, or the faith of their friends and family, but sometimes he just acted. Jesus healed by touch or by a word and he also healed from a distance. We cannot put God in a box and say that he always works in a certain way. Share examples of God working in surprising ways in your lives or in the lives of people you know or have read about.

- The religious leaders saw healing as part of a doctor's profession and hence as work, which was forbidden on the sabbath. Read Exodus 20:8–11, one of the Ten Commandments. How can we keep Sunday, our sabbath rest, special? How can we prevent it from becoming burdensome with rules and regulations? Rest and recreation are essential for healthy living. Share ways in which you have achieved or attempt to achieve a healthy work/rest/play balance.

- Being legalistic can prevent us from seeing what would truly please God and can lead us to having lopsided priorities. Can you give examples of times when you have seen this happen?

- Jesus said, 'Do not think that I have come to abolish the Law or the Prophets; I have not come to abolish them but to fulfil them' (Matthew 5:17, NIV). It was the additional rules and regulations that Jesus criticised because they had the power to take the joy out of the lives of his people and therefore to harm their perception of and relationship with God. The rules that God has given for our lives are there to protect us and to give us life in its fullness. For example, if we do not covet (crave what others have), we are free to delight in what we have and experience the joy of gratitude. Can you think of other examples of God's laws bringing freedom? Can you think of examples where human rules bring bondage?

- When we come to Christ, he changes us step by step, dealing with what cripples us spiritually, mentally and emotionally, enabling us to 'stand straight'. If you feel able, share ways in which you have learnt or are learning to 'stand straight'. We can walk with our heads held high in spite of our past because of Christ's work in our lives.

- The woman had the choice of whether or not to step towards Jesus. In our adversities we can come nearer to Jesus or walk away; our circumstances can make us more like Jesus or can spoil our journey with him. The choice to step towards him is ours.

- What simple God-given pleasures give you joy?

- What have you learnt of Jesus in this study? He desires ongoing growth and release for us as the Holy Spirit works within us. 'Now the Lord is the Spirit, and where the Spirit of the Lord is, there is freedom. And we… are being transformed into his likeness with ever-increasing glory, which comes from the Lord, who is the Spirit' (2 Corinthians 3:17–18, NIV).

Conclusion

Take time to pray through your findings. What might God be saying to you? Is anything particularly relevant to your life at the moment? Write down what you have learnt and refer back to it regularly in the days ahead so that it becomes part of your thinking, reacting and lifestyle.

Jesus and
the Gentile woman of faith

Introduction

- Read Matthew 15:21–28 and Mark 7:24–30.

- Ask God to speak to you through this episode. You could use the words from Psalm 119:124: 'Let your love dictate how you deal with me; teach me from your textbook on life' (*THE MESSAGE*).

- Sit back, relax and close your eyes. Imagine the scene as someone reads out the monologue.

Monologue

It was my desperation that brought me to Jesus, for my daughter was behaving so strangely that I believed she was possessed. The agony of watching her in this state, of feeling both so helpless and so guilty, had left me depleted. I had heard that the Jewish rabbi, Jesus, whom everyone spoke of, had arrived and was close by. I had marvelled at the stories of his healings and knew that this was my opportunity. Having made arrangements for my daughter to be looked after, I slipped from my home and made for the house in which it was rumoured he was staying. I peered through the door; Jesus was there.

It took so much courage to approach him. You see, I am from Canaan and my very appearance marks me as different. I had only to open my mouth and utter a sentence for my accent to be recognised. But my love for my daughter outweighed my fear. I moved towards Jesus until I was right in front of him. It was now or never.

'Lord, have mercy on me. O Son of David! My daughter is possessed by an evil spirit. She is in torment.'

My words gushed out—all that pent-up emotion, such hope and fear in so few words. Jesus looked at me but gave not a word of reply. In that look I saw that he had taken in the situation and understood what I was feeling. A flicker of hope rose in my heart, enough to ask again and again for his help. I could see that I was a cause of annoyance, maybe even embarrassment, to his disciples, who were beginning to cluster around Jesus protectively, trying to block my access to him. Eventually one of them said to Jesus, 'Tell her to go. She is irritating us with all her begging.'

He stepped out of the gathering circle around him and came close to me, his gentle eyes fixed on my face. 'I want you to understand, my first calling is to help the people of Israel, God's lost sheep.'

I fell at his feet, overwhelmed by his presence, his purity, his power. 'Lord, I know you can help. Please, please have mercy on me.'

At that moment a dog sidled up to Jesus, rubbing against him. Jesus looked down with affection and ruffled the fur on its head. 'We don't give the food that is meant for our children to the dogs,' he said gently.

I knew what he was driving at, could sense his pain in seeing my agony. Thinking of our own family table, I replied, 'True, but the dogs *do* eat the crumbs that fall from the table off the children's plates.'

At this, his face broke into a smile and he chuckled, 'Good answer! You have so much faith. Your request is granted. Go home, for the demon has left your daughter and she is asking for you.'

I did not need to be told twice. I ran from the room all the way home. As I entered, I saw her lying in bed completely at peace. I knew that the demon had left her at the very moment Jesus had spoken those words. Tears of gratitude flowed down my cheeks. As I held her in my arms, I wondered whether Jesus had planned to heal her all along. Why had he waited? Was it to show me the extent of my faith? Or was it to show the others that although he must minister to the Jews first, he had also come for the Gentiles who believed in him?

Reflection and discussion

- Did any words or phrases stand out for you? Before further discussion, read the passage again in a different translation or paraphrase of the Bible.

- On first reading, the words of Jesus and his attitude to the woman can seem harsh. Has the monologue given you any fresh insights into the passage?

- We can learn about our communication with God from the Gentile woman.

  - She was not afraid to continue asking for help, even when no answer was forthcoming. Read the parable of the persistent widow in Luke 18:1–8. Are there any hints as to why we sometimes have to persist in prayer? Share times in your lives when you have waited for a much-prayed prayer to be answered. If you are able, share prayers that you are still waiting to see answered.

  - We need not worry if we end up repeating many of our prayers, often on a daily basis, for these prayers show that we are seeking God's help in the everyday ebb and flow of our lives. In them we acknowledge not only our human need but also our faith in God's empowerment. Share daily 'maintenance' prayers that you pray.

– The Gentile woman was not afraid to argue her case with Jesus. She was honest. We read examples of honest prayers in the Psalms. Although we come before God with reverence, we can come in total honesty, even 'wrestling' with him, as Jacob did (Genesis 32:22–32). Is there anything that you have wrestled over with God that you could share?

– In her desire to be heard by Jesus, the Gentile woman did not worry about what others thought of her. Has fear of what others may think of you affected your responses to God, such as the way you worship in public or the way you pray with others? Such fear can prevent the growth of your faith. How can this be overcome? Share your thoughts and experiences.

■ Even the Son of God had priorities, for the need around him was without end. This episode shows us the importance of having priorities and having enough flexibility to amend them. Take a few moments of quiet to consider your current priorities. Is too much activity preventing you from fulfilling your God-given priorities? Where could you cut back? Have you lost your sense of purpose amid too many demands from others or from pressures within yourself? Once you have had some time to think through these questions alone, honestly share your ideas and struggles.

■ We have the example of Jesus in putting limits on our activity and in not succumbing to the pressure of others. However, sometimes an interruption to our plans can be the leading of God. In this passage the disciples failed to recognise that leading. Do you have any examples of God's 'interruptions' that you could share?

- We can have confidence that when God's answer to our request is 'wait', there will be reasons for it. 'Waiting' seasons develop our faith, patience and endurance. Romans 8:28 says, 'And we know that God causes everything to work together for the good of those who love God and are called according to his purpose for them.' Share times when you have been in a waiting season.

- We can also use these life experiences to encourage and support others. 2 Corinthians 1:4 says, 'He comforts us in all our troubles so that we can comfort others. When they are troubled, we will be able to give them the same comfort God has given us.'

- What new insights into the character of Jesus have you gained from this study? How will this make a difference to your relationship with him?

Conclusion

Take time to pray through your findings. What might God be saying to you? Is anything particularly relevant to your life at the moment? Write down what you have learnt and refer back to it regularly in the days ahead so that it becomes part of your thinking, reacting and lifestyle.

Jesus and the woman who dared to touch his robe

Introduction

- Read Luke 8:40–50.

- Ask God to speak to you through this episode. You could use the words from Psalm 119:132: 'Come and have mercy on me as is your way with those who love you' (LB).

- Sit back, relax and close your eyes. Imagine the scene as someone reads out the monologue.

Monologue

He was my last hope, this Jesus. We had heard so much about him and were waiting for him to land. We lined the shore, watching the fishing boats that would bring him and his disciples to us. News of his healings, his ability to cast out demons, even raise the dead, had spread far and wide. These brought me new hope: if he could do miracles for other people, perhaps he could do one for me.

I should not really have been there among the crowd. You see, I was ritually unclean, always ritually unclean, because of my constant flow of blood; untouchable, lest others be contaminated. I lived in a shadowland. Oh, how I longed for touch, for affirmation, but there was none. I had endured a twelve-year struggle looking for a solution—hopes raised by a possible cure, money found to pay for it, and hopes dashed once again. The day had come when there was no money left and no hope left.

Then I heard about Jesus, and something in me began to whisper words of new hope, new possibility. So there I was, heavily veiled to avoid recognition, squeezing my way through the heaving throng to reach him.

As he disembarked, there was a clamour of voices wanting his attention and then a sudden silence as the leader of the synagogue, Jairus, stepped forward. But this was not the Jairus we knew, full of self-control. Here was a desperate man, on the ground at Jesus' feet, begging, pleading with him to come to his home. By this time I was very near, near enough to hear that his beautiful twelve-year-old daughter, Talitha, was dying. I could remember her birth, for she was born as my illness started. Her twelve years of vitality had contrasted with my twelve years of exhaustion. Now, here we were, both in need of Jesus. But how could I ask for help when her case was a matter of life and death?

I couldn't, so, with the rest of the crowd, I stepped back to let them pass. He came so close, I felt an overwhelming urge to reach out, to touch him, for hadn't he healed with a touch? What if *I* made the connection? I took one step behind him, touched the very fringe of his robe and then merged back into the crowd as quickly as I could.

I knew immediately that I was different, as only a sick person, suddenly feeling well, can know. I was outwardly the same, yet inwardly totally transformed. Joy welled up within me; depths of gratitude bubbled from my heart. I wanted to rush from the crowd, to run, to dance! Then I noticed that Jesus had stopped.

'Who touched me?' He asked.

Fear gripped me and I took another step back while those around me denied touching him. Jairus' face was pinched with agony at the delay.

One of the disciples replied, 'Master, the crowds are pressing up against us. It's not surprising that someone touched you.'

'No,' Jesus said, 'It was a deliberate touch. I felt power leave me.'

I could not remain hidden: valuable time was being lost. Jesus needed to get to Talitha. Trembling, I fell on my knees at his feet. I looked up and saw that he was waiting for me to speak. I knew that by my touch I had made him ceremonially unclean. I stammered out my story, aware that the silent crowd was listening intently and would be angered by my action. Would Jesus condemn my daring, unlawful act? But when I got to tell of my healing, joy flowed and my thanks came from a full heart.

I shall never forget his words of affirmation: 'Daughter, your faith has made you well. Go in peace.'

'Daughter…' I was once more an acceptable part of the family of Abraham. 'Peace…' How I longed for that, as much as I had longed for health. The anxiety and shame I had carried throughout the illness lifted. I was free.

The moment of intimacy was broken by a wail from Jairus. He had been told the news of his daughter's death. There would be no point in bringing the teacher, Jesus, to his home.

Jesus went over to Jairus, took him by the shoulders and said, 'Don't be afraid. Have faith. She will be healed.'

I believed him.

Reflection and discussion

- Did any words or phrases stand out for you? Before further discussion, read the passage again in a different translation or paraphrase of the Bible.

- The woman in this encounter had suffered for twelve years. We can imagine her growing isolation and loneliness. Do we find it difficult to 'hang in' with friends when the difficult times that they are experiencing are protracted, or when their relationship with us becomes restricted by their limitations and struggles, or when there seems to be no progress in their circumstances in spite of our prayers and care? Share your thoughts. Read Proverbs 17:17: 'A friend is always loyal.'

- Are there times when you have known a growing isolation or loneliness? Read Hebrews 13:5: 'God has said, "I will never fail you. I will never abandon you".'

- Like the woman in the monologue, we can feel that the requests we make to God are less important than those of others. While we should be prayerfully mindful of the needs of others and of world issues, this episode shows us that no request of our own is too small to bring to Jesus. How does this knowledge affect our prayer life?

- Jesus chose to draw attention to the fact that he had been touched and demanded to know who was responsible. Why do you think he did this? Was he showing the crowd that no one should be overlooked and that everyone deserves respect? Possibly it was so that he could have a personal encounter with the woman and let her know that he was responsible for the healing, rather than magical qualities in the cloak itself. Or was it to let her family and acquaintances know that she was healed so that they would accept her back into the community? Perhaps it was so that the woman could have the experience of sharing her faith, of putting into words what Jesus had done for her. Jesus brought the woman out of her comfort zone in order to bless her and others. When has God taken you out of your comfort zone?

- Take a few moments to share healing that Jesus has brought to you, whether of body, soul or spirit. This will be faith-building for you and encouraging for the rest of the group.

- The woman was on the fringe of Jewish society. Which people in our society are overlooked? What can we do as individuals or groups to value them?

- Jesus saw her need for peace as well as healing. Pray that you will be aware of the spiritual needs in others that may be hidden behind other issues.

- What have you learnt of Jesus in this study?

Conclusion

Take time to pray through your findings. What might God be saying to you? Is anything particularly relevant to your life at the moment? Write down what you have learnt and refer back to it regularly in the days ahead so that it becomes part of your thinking, reacting and lifestyle.

Jesus and the woman caught in adultery

Introduction

- Read John 8:1–11.

- Ask God to speak to you through this episode. You could use the words from Psalm 119:66: 'Teach me knowledge and good judgment, for I believe in your commands' (NIV 1984).

- Sit back, relax and close your eyes. Imagine the scene as someone reads out the monologue.

Monologue

I felt a rough hand on my shoulder, pushing me towards Jesus, causing me to stumble and fall at his feet. I kept my eyes down, knowing that the gaze of the whole crowd was fixed on me.

'Teacher,' one of the Pharisees said, 'this woman was caught in the act of adultery. The Law of Moses says that she should be stoned to death. What do you say?'

There was a complete hush. Jesus was trapped, I knew it. How could he disagree with the Law of Moses? There was no alternative; he would have to condemn me to death. My body started to shake uncontrollably.

As I crouched there, my face in my hands, the silence was broken by a scratching sound. I raised my head slightly to see what was going on and realised that Jesus had bent over and was writing in the dust with his finger, quite close to me.

What was he writing? Only the teachers and I were close enough to see. It was the commandments that God had given to Moses, starting with 'You must have no other God before me.'

The teachers of the law and the Pharisees grew impatient, demanding a reply to their question, but Jesus just continued writing: 'You must not make for yourself an idol of any kind.'

'Answer us,' one shouted.

'You must not misuse the name of the Lord your God,' he wrote.

Then he stood up and looked straight at them. 'The one who has never sinned should be the first to throw a stone.'

At that moment I heard a wail and my heart was torn apart. It was the cry of my son. Instinctively my eyes turned in the direction of the cry and there he was, standing next to my husband, clinging to him, his face streaked with tears. My eyes met those of my husband for just a second, and I saw there the agony of a betrayed man. I saw Jesus look at them too; his eyes were filled with deep compassion, as if he understood pain and betrayal.

He bent over again and continued to write. 'Remember to observe the Sabbath day by keeping it holy.'

I heard desperate shouts for mercy and realised that they were coming from my own lips. In self-protection I curled my body over my knees, wrapping my hands around my head, and awaited the first blow.

Silence. Only the scratching of the writing was audible. 'Honour your father and mother.'

The stillness was broken by the sound of footsteps, at first near and then fading away into the distance.

Silence again. Then the scratching continued. 'You shall not murder.' There were more footsteps.

I hardly dared read what Jesus wrote next. 'You shall not commit adultery.' My shame and my pain welled up inside me. I wanted to talk to this rabbi, to explain and try to justify myself. I had not set out to be unfaithful to my husband. It was years of loneliness and the absence of gentle words, loving touch or shared laughter—and then the discovery of all this in the arms of another man. I had taken a terrible risk to feel alive and wanted. The words remained written in the dust in front of me, so close that I could touch them.

I sensed movement behind me. Surely now that they could see these words, the first stone would be thrown. But there was not a thud. Not a word.

So the silence and the scratching continued. 'You must not steal,' Jesus wrote.

All the while, the crowd was motionless, while behind me the footsteps continued, at first loud and then dying away.

'You must not testify falsely against your neighbour.' Bit by bit, I straightened my body; I dared to turn to look. They had left. Every single one of the religious leaders had gone. On the edge of the crowd I could see my husband and son waiting. Waiting for what?

'You must not covet.' Jesus stood up, looking at me. Is that not what I had been doing? Coveting what I did not have? Jesus slowly took in the scene around him: the crowd, my family, the empty space where the Pharisees had stood.

He said gently to me, 'Where are those who accused you? Does not even one of them condemn you?'

'No, Lord,' I whispered.

With great authority and for all to hear, Jesus said, 'Neither do I condemn you. Now go and sin no more.'

Reflection and discussion

- Did any words or phrases stand out for you? Before further discussion, read the passage again in a different translation or paraphrase of the Bible.

- We do not know how the story ended. Did the woman's husband have the grace to extend forgiveness? We can only imagine.

- In Deuteronomy 22:22 the law stated that the man and the woman caught in adultery must die; in this scene, only the woman was brought before Jesus. In his patriarchal society, Jesus' treatment of women was revolutionary.

- In our age of political correctness, how do we maintain God's absolutes? Are there practical ways in which we can stand up for God's absolutes without being judgmental? Jesus said, 'Do not judge others, and you will not be judged' (Matthew 7:1). He demonstrated a perfect balance between justice and mercy. How can we aim to do the same, both as individuals and as groups?

- This event demonstrates God's grace. Jesus was the only one without sin—the one who could have thrown the stone—but he neither condemned the woman nor condoned her actions. Instead he poured out his grace on her, giving her the opportunity to live a different life. Read 1 John 1:8–9: 'If we claim we have no sin, we are only fooling ourselves and not living in the truth. But if we confess our sins to him, he is faithful and just to forgive us our sins and to cleanse us from all wickedness.' God extends the same grace to each of us. Take some time in personal reflection to bring any areas of your lives to God where you need forgiveness and to experience his grace.

- Jesus always sought relationship: his encounters with individuals always took on a personal nature. When asked what was the most important commandment in the Law of Moses, he replied, 'You must love the Lord your God with all your heart, all your soul, and all your mind' (Matthew 22:37). He desires a love relationship with each of us, out of which we respond in obedience. How is this different from a legalistic following of Christ?

- Jesus gave a second commandment: 'Love your neighbour as yourself.' He added, 'The entire law and all the demands of the prophets are based on these two commandments' (Matthew 22:39–40). We would like to receive mercy and so we must give mercy. This was demonstrated to the watching crowd, as they saw the Pharisees and the teachers of the law gradually departing, for they too had sinned and needed God's mercy. We would like to receive forgiveness, so we must forgive others. We must also learn to forgive ourselves. If appropriate, share ways in which you have been enabled to forgive others and yourself.

- We see the wisdom of Christ in this encounter. We are advised to seek after wisdom in the book of Proverbs. Read Proverbs 3:13–18. What are the results of wise living? Do we pray regularly for those we love and care for to gain wisdom? What opportunities do we have to pass on wisdom to others by how we live and what we say? Share examples of times when you have gained from the wisdom of others.

- How can you know Jesus more as a result of this study? How will this knowledge affect your life, attitudes and relationships?

Conclusion

Take time to pray through your findings. What might God be saying to you? Is anything particularly relevant to your life at the moment? Write down what you have learnt and refer back to it regularly in the days ahead so that it becomes part of your thinking, reacting and lifestyle.

Salome, mother of James and John

Introduction

■ Read Mark 15:40; 16:1; Matthew 27:55–56 and John 19:25.

■ It is probable that the mother of the sons of Zebedee, James and John, was Salome. It has even been suggested that James and John could have been cousins of Jesus, if the unnamed woman in John 19:25, Jesus' mother's sister, was Salome. Here I have assumed that Salome is the mother of James and John, but have not imagined her as the aunt of Jesus.

■ Read Mark 1:16–20; 3:17; Luke 8:1–3; 9:49–56 and Matthew 20:20–28. Some of these passages could be read before the monologue and some of them afterwards.

■ Ask God to speak to you through this episode. You could use the words from Psalm 119:125: 'I'm your servant—help me understand what that means, the inner meaning of your instructions' (THE MESSAGE).

■ Sit back, relax and close your eyes. Imagine the scene as someone reads out the monologue.

Monologue

In many ways it had not been a hard decision for Zebedee and me to make. Our two sons were headstrong and determined and we had watched their growing commitment to the rabbi, Jesus of Nazareth. One day, Zebedee had returned home and told me that Jesus had walked along the edge of the lake while they were sitting in the boat repairing nets. They had listened as Jesus called Andrew and Peter from their fishing, telling them that he would show them how to fish for people. At the time, I wondered what that was supposed to mean, but as the weeks and months unfurled, I grew to understand.

Jesus had then walked along the shore nearer to Zebedee's boat and called out to James and John. Immediately they had jumped out of the boat and gone after Jesus. Peter and Andrew were partners and close friends of James and John, so it did not surprise me that they were in this together.

We began to see less of James and John, for they would travel to other towns with Jesus and we would hear news of Jesus' authoritative preaching and of wonderful healings.

Eventually I was to go, too. That was the decision that Zebedee and I had to make. Would we let our boys go alone or should I go and keep an eye on them? My husband's business was successful and he had hired help, so he could manage without our two lads. We knew the temperaments of our boys: they were hot-headed and high-spirited. So as I said, really the decision was easy. Also, I knew that other women were joining Jesus' group, women like me who could afford to support Jesus and his followers. It would be an adventure and I would enjoy their company.

It turned out to be far more than an adventure.

Jesus chose twelve of his supporters to be particularly close to him, and I was proud that James and John were among this group, along with Andrew and Simon, whom Jesus now called Peter. He had a name for my two sons too: Boanerges, the Sons of Thunder. They earned this name— even I, as their mother, had to admit it! They were so keen to follow Jesus and were fiercely loyal to him. They wanted to see the kingdom of heaven come on earth in great power, but sometimes their enthusiasm was misdirected and Jesus had to rebuke them. On one occasion, they saw someone casting out demons in Jesus' name and tried to stop him. When they told Jesus what had happened, Jesus said, 'Don't stop him! Anyone who is not against you is for you.'

What did he mean? The words of Jesus often surprised me, staying in my mind where I would chew them over.

On another occasion, the people in a Samaritan village would not allow us to stay there because we were on our way to Jerusalem. James and John were indignant and, knowing the power available to them, wanted to bring down fire from heaven to burn up the Samaritans. Now you understand the name Jesus gave them! That resulted in another rebuke from Jesus.

I had begun to notice that Jesus seemed to have special relationships with my two lads and Peter. John, my youngest son, seemed particularly close to Jesus. I was immensely proud. There were times when Jesus would take just the three of them with him, such as when Jairus' daughter was raised from the dead.[27] Then there was that other time when they were gone for a long time up a mountain with Jesus. They wouldn't say what had happened up there, even with my probing. I knew that it had been something momentous, though, for I had never seen my sons so sub-dued. Occasionally I would see Peter, James and John in serious conversation together, but if anyone drew near they stopped speaking.[28]

So perhaps it was watching these incidents from a dis-tance that led me to the conclusion that James and John were to be very important in the kingdom of God. I began to speak to them about this and encouraged them to discuss their position with Jesus. They were ambitious young men and I was ambitious for them. I see that now.

Somehow, even after all we had seen of the selfless life of Jesus, we were still out to gain positions of importance. Somehow we had missed the point. The words Jesus had spoken to us of his betrayal, death and resurrection on the third day were beyond our grasp. All we could see were the crowd following us and the wonderful healings.

It was after one of these discussions with James and John that we decided to approach Jesus. I walked up to our Lord and knelt respectfully at his feet, James and John behind me. 'I have something to ask you, Lord,' I said.

'What is your request?' Jesus asked me.

'In your kingdom, please let my two sons sit in places of honour next to you, one on your right and the other on your left,' I replied.

There was a long silence and then Jesus said to me, 'You don't know what you are asking.' Then he looked keenly at James and John, saying, 'Are you able to drink from the bitter cup of suffering I am about to drink?'

Oh, my boys! Always impetuous! 'Yes, we are able,' they replied. Little did we realise then what was to unfold in all of our lives.

Jesus spoke sadly to them: 'You will indeed drink from my bitter cup. But I have no right to say who will sit on my right or my left. My Father has prepared those places for the ones he has chosen.'

Shame filled my heart as I realised the enormity of what I had requested and my pride in pushing my sons forward.

That was not the end of it. The other disciples had heard

enough of the conversation to feel indignant and resentful. My shame deepened, for I had caused further rivalry, sown seeds for another dispute to divide the disciples.

Jesus called us together and said, 'The rulers of this world lord it over their people and we see every day the officials flaunting their authority over those under them. But among you it will be different. Whoever wants to be a leader among you must be your servant and whoever wants to be first among you must become your slave. For even the Son of Man came not to be served but to serve others and to give his life as a ransom for many.'

I had much to mull over that night. 'Son of Man': that was a title I had heard Jesus use before to refer to himself. 'The Son of Man came to serve others.' Wasn't that what we saw Jesus do each day? But what did he mean by 'give his life as a ransom for many?'

We had misunderstood so much, my boys and I. From then on, we began to understand that following Jesus was not about position, lording it over others, but about serving others. I started to see a change in James and John: they seemed to look for opportunities to help the Lord in any way they could. My pride in them became gentler and less demanding, for I recognised that the future was not mine to control. John in particular would always try to stay as near to Jesus as he could. Perhaps he sensed more than the others that there was trouble ahead.

Reflection and discussion

■ Did any words or phrases stand out for you? Before further discussion, read some or all of the passages again in a different translation or paraphrase of the Bible.

- Consider what Jesus meant by the words, 'Anyone who is not against you is for you' (Luke 9:50). How are these words relevant to us in today's culture?

- In this episode we see the ambition of Salome, James and John. Is there a place for ambition for oneself or for others? How can we aim high and develop our gifts and the gifts of those within our care without being overly ambitious? Should we be ambitious for our children as mothers, aunts or grandmothers?

- Read Philippians 2:3–4: 'Do nothing out of selfish ambition or vain conceit, but in humility consider others better than yourselves. Each of you should look not only to your own interests, but also to the interests of others' (NIV 1984). The parable of the talents directs us to make the most of the resources and abilities of which we are stewards (Matthew 25:14–30). How do we balance this with the verses from Philippians?

- There was rivalry among the disciples over which of them was the greatest. They had not yet grasped the heart of Jesus' message: 'The Son of Man did not come to be served, but to serve' (Matthew 20:28, NIV). The disciples were still under the misunderstanding that their relationship with Jesus would result in status, and they were vying for the top positions. In this episode we see how self-seeking eats away at unity, for the ambition of Salome, James and John resulted in conflict with the other disciples. Read Colossians 3:12–15. What advice are we given that will help us to live in unity in our families, churches and communities?

- What does this episode and other verses in the Bible have to say about pride and humility? See Proverbs 8:13; Psalm 138:6; Matthew 11:29 and James 4:10.

- What does it mean in practice to serve rather than to 'lord' it over others? How do we do this when we are in positions of leadership and authority?

- Jesus always accepted his followers as they were but gave them opportunities, through his teaching and example, to change. He saw the potential within James and John while they were still immature in their faith. We, too, are all works in progress. How does this knowledge affect our dealings with ourselves and with others, particularly those entrusted to our care? Be encouraged by the promise, 'God, who began the good work within you, will continue his work until it is finally finished on the day when Christ Jesus returns' (Philippians 1:6).

- In the monologue, Salome mulls over the words of Jesus, trying to get to the heart of their meaning. One method of pondering on the words of Jesus is *Lectio Divina* ('sacred reading'): after reading a passage, focus on a phrase or word from the text, meditating (reflecting and pondering) on it. Respond with prayer and then wait in silence, resting in God. Through this, 'he will empower you with inner strength through his Spirit. Then Christ will make his home in your hearts as you trust in him. Your roots will grow down into God's love and keep you strong' (Ephesians 3:16–17). If members of your group have used this method or another way of thinking about words of scripture, it would be helpful if they could share their experience with the group.

- James and John were to drink the 'cup of suffering' alluded to by Jesus in this episode. James was martyred for his faith: 'It was about this time that King Herod arrested some who belonged to the church, intending to persecute them. He had James, the brother of John, put to death with the sword' (Acts 12:1–2, NIV). Many scholars believe that John lived to an old age and was the John who received the visions recorded in the book of Revelation while in exile: 'I, John, your brother and companion in the suffering and kingdom and patient endurance that are ours in Jesus, was on the island of Patmos because of the word of God and the testimony of Jesus' (Revelation 1:9, NIV).

Conclusion

Take time to pray through your findings. What might God be saying to you? Is anything particularly relevant to your life at the moment? Write down what you have learnt and refer back to it regularly in the days ahead so that it becomes part of your thinking, reacting and lifestyle.

Jesus' visit to Bethany: Martha

This and the following study are both based on the same biblical incident and could be covered in one session, depending on the time available. If so, the conclusion could be left until the end of the second study.

Introduction

- Read Luke 10:38–42.

- Ask God to speak to you through this episode. You could use the words from Psalm 119:105: 'Your word is a lamp to guide my feet and a light for my path.'

- Sit back, relax and close your eyes. Imagine the scene as someone reads out the monologue.

Monologue

There was so much to think about, so much to get done. I had seen a crowd gathering and had gone over to see what was going on. Not much in Bethany missed my eyes or ears! There stood Jesus; at last the great rabbi had come to our village. I edged and, dare I say it, pushed my way to the front of the crowd. When there was a moment, I told Jesus that my brother, my sister and I had talked about him and how much we wanted to meet him. Would he like to come for dinner?

He smiled at me, a smile that went to the core of my being. It was as if he had been expecting me, as if he knew me... or wanted to know me. I took the smile as a 'yes';

then, with horror, I realised that it wouldn't just be the rabbi who would arrive at our home at the end of a busy day, but his disciples too! Suddenly a dinner for four had become a dinner for sixteen.

There was no time to listen or to watch the goings on. I had to get cracking! By the time I had reached home, I had the whole meal planned; I knew what I would do and what I would get Mary to do. I would go round to our neighbours, borrowing all the extra plates and cups we needed, and Mary would start on the cooking.

The trouble was that she had other ideas—if you can call her daydreaming 'having other ideas'. She couldn't seem to concentrate on the tasks in hand and kept gazing down the street. When Lazarus eventually brought Jesus and his friends in, we welcomed them, and that was the last I saw of Mary. I struggled on, rushing here and there, flustered, hot and bothered. Occasionally I heard a snippet of what he was saying. The words 'kingdom of God' and 'love the Lord your God' caught my attention but were crowded out by the next job.

Eventually something in me cracked. Pushing my way into the circle around Jesus, I asked, 'Lord, does it seem unfair to you that my sister is sitting here while I do all the work? Ask her to come and help me.'

I shall never forget his response or the tenderness in his voice as he called me his 'dear Martha'. 'You are so wound up, worrying over the details! There is only one thing worth concerning yourself over, and Mary has discovered it. It won't be taken away from her.'

It wasn't that he had refused my request that affected me so deeply; it was his total understanding of me and his insight into how I ticked. You see, the meal was only the superficial issue; the real issue was my inability to be inwardly still, my constant need to be doing, my lack of inner silence. The inner me is always thinking and planning, fretting and worrying, restless. So I miss opportunities to listen, opportunities to be refreshed.

That very day I had missed hearing Jesus speak to the crowds and then missed hearing him speak in the quietness of our own home. In those few words Jesus had described me, but without passing judgment; he had opened up the possibility of a new way of being, a new set of priorities, a new me.

The rest of that evening was a delight to me. I listened intently to Jesus as I served. How I enjoyed seeing the pleasure of those hungry men as they ate our food and relaxed! It was the start of a deep friendship between Jesus, his disciples and my family.

Reflection and discussion

■ Did any words or phrases stand out for you? Before further discussion, read the passage again in a different translation or paraphrase of the Bible.

■ Resentments can creep into our lives so easily and can be harmful both to our relationships and to our spiritual growth. Can you think of a current or past relationship where this is or has been the case? If appropriate, share your experiences and support each other in finding ways forward. The following way of resolving conflict may be useful:

– Address the issue rather than attacking the person.

– Identify your feelings rather than blaming the person.

– Suggest a resolution and ask the person if they can co-operate with it.

- Give positive feedback when he or she cooperates.

- Remember the deep love that Jesus has both for you and for the other person concerned. In the extract we have meditated on, Jesus shows his love for both Mary and Martha.

■ We all have outward demands on our attention—family, homes, work, friendships and other commitments—and yet our inner resources are depleted much more easily than we realise. We have to learn to pace ourselves and set limits. Think of ways in which you have done this or areas in which you need to do it. Share them and support each other in finding possible solutions.

■ Even if our lives are reasonably paced, it is possible to be inwardly restless and fretful, like Martha. Pause to identify these feelings within yourself and to recognise the need to listen to God in order to gain insight and direction. What helps you to find inner stillness? Share your ideas.

■ Read John 11:20–27. We can take encouragement from the observation that Martha's restlessness did not prevent her from having a close relationship with Jesus. We see this relationship both in her honesty when speaking to Jesus and in her deep faith in him as the Messiah, the Son of God, which sustained her even in the face of personal tragedy.

■ What have you learnt from this study of Jesus as 'the Messiah, the Son of God, the one who has come into the world from God' (Martha's words in John 11:27)?

Conclusion

Take time to pray through your findings. What might God be saying to you? Is anything particularly relevant to your life at the moment? Write down what you have learnt and refer back to it regularly in the days ahead so that it becomes part of your thinking, reacting and lifestyle.

Jesus' visit to Bethany: Mary

Introduction

- Read Luke 10:38–42.

- Ask God to speak to you through this episode. You could use the words from Psalm 119:114: 'You're my place of quiet retreat; I wait for your Word to renew me' (THE MESSAGE).

- Sit back, relax and close your eyes. Imagine the scene as someone reads out the monologue.

Monologue

Martha rushed into the house in great excitement. 'I've just met Jesus, the man everyone has been talking about. He's here in Bethany. I've invited him for dinner.'

My heart leapt: we had heard so much about Jesus from people travelling through Bethany. Two of his disciples had stayed nearby, teaching and performing miracles in his name. My brother, Lazarus, Martha and I had spoken of him in the evenings, wondering if he could be the long-awaited Messiah. Now he was here and coming into our home! Martha had already collected all we needed from the neighbours and had started busying herself with food preparations, talking about what she needed to do next and what I could do to help. I helped her but found myself drawn to the door over and over again, looking out for him. As our mother had always told us, I was the dreamer, the reflective one, and Martha was the activist.

At last I saw a group of men approaching our home. We welcomed them according to our custom, washing the dust from their feet and drying them. Once Jesus was reclining with his friends around him, I positioned myself near his feet, ignoring the hostile glances that I received from his disciples. I knew that, as a woman, I should not be sitting at the feet of a rabbi, learning from him, but I was desperate to drink in all he had to say. He spoke of God's kingdom, of recovery of sight to the blind, of lepers healed and the deaf hearing. He told stories, such wonderful stories. I listened as he explained their meaning to his disciples who were asking questions. When he looked at me, his eyes were gentle, welcoming, accepting, as if I had every right to be there among a group of men. Then he spoke of God wanting our love, not just our obedience. That was new to me and, before I knew what I was doing, I had asked a question about how I could love God and be part of his kingdom.

I was so lost in his words that I had forgotten Martha, the dinner and her need for my help—that is, until her voice filled a lapse in our conversation: 'Lord, ask my sister to help me! It must seem unfair to you that I should do all the work.'

I blushed with the shame of being criticised in front of such a crowd of people and the thought of being reprimanded by this rabbi. I was fast realising that he was far more than a rabbi. Could the Anointed One be sitting in front of me? But no reprimand came.

With smiling eyes and a light tone of voice, he said to Martha, 'My dear Martha, you are so wound up, worrying over the details! There is only one thing worth concerning yourself over, and Mary has discovered it. It won't be taken away from her.'

So I sat and listened, we ate, we spoke, and by the end

of the evening we three, Lazarus, Martha and I, had made a friend above all friends. How I looked forward to Jesus' visits! His acceptance and his life-giving words transformed me.

Reflection and discussion

- Did any words or phrases stand out for you? Before further discussion, read the passage again in a different translation or paraphrase of the Bible.

- Mary shows us the importance of developing the reflective inner life. Jesus, in this episode, shows that time spent listening to him is essential rather than an option. What helps us develop our spiritual inner life?

- Are there times in your life when circumstances have enabled or even forced you to re-examine your life and focus on the inner life of the Spirit?

- How can we balance the Martha and Mary aspects of our characters?

- The monologue shows Mary's wonder at having the Messiah in her home. The possibility of intimacy with God is amazing. Jesus shows us that God is not distant or critical, but *wants* a relationship with us. We can lose the wonder of this truth because of its familiarity. How can it be recaptured?

- Read John 14:16–17a: 'And I will ask the Father, and he will give you another Advocate, who will never leave you. He is the Holy Spirit, who leads into all truth.' God's plan was that once his Son left this earth, his followers would enjoy the intimacy of the Holy Spirit, who is both in us and with us: 'You know him, for he lives with you and will be in you' (v. 17b, NIV). 'But when the Father sends the

Advocate as my representative—that is, the Holy Spirit—he will teach you everything and will remind you of everything I have told you' (v. 26). What are we promised? In what ways have you experienced it?

■ Jesus is seen to be enjoying friendship in this episode. God has always wanted a relationship of friendship with us: in Isaiah 41:8 God refers to Abraham as his friend, and in John 15:15 Jesus tells his disciples, 'Now you are my friends, since I have told you everything the Father told me.' On our spiritual journey we are developing a friendship with God. Friendships always carry the potential for growth. What have you learnt of God the Father, God the Son and God the Holy Spirit that will help you grow in your friendship with him through this study?

Conclusion

Take time to pray through your findings. What might God be saying to you? Is anything particularly relevant to your life at the moment? Write down what you have learnt and refer back to it regularly in the days ahead so that it becomes part of your thinking, reacting and lifestyle.

Jesus and Martha at the raising of Lazarus (Part 1)

This and the following study are both based on the same biblical incident and could be covered in one session, depending on the time available. If so, the conclusion could be left until the end of the second study.

Introduction

- Read John 11:1–46. You may like to read the first 29 verses before the monologue and the rest of the verses after it.

- Ask God to speak to you through this episode. You could use the words from Psalm 119:156: 'Lord, how great is your mercy; oh, give me back my life again' (LB).

- Sit back, relax and close your eyes. Imagine the scene as someone reads the monologue.

Monologue

Mary and I had had our differences, but the moment Lazarus became ill, we were united in our determination to care for him to the best of our ability. But it was not the ability to care for him that was needed; it was the skill to make him well, and that we did not have. Our Lord did, though.

As Lazarus deteriorated, our anxiety grew and we discussed the possibility of sending a messenger to fetch Jesus. We were not keen to disturb him or draw him away from his wonderful work of teaching and ministering to others, but Jesus loved Lazarus. Surely he would want to help us? At the same time, we knew that there were those here in Judea who would stone our Lord to death. Indeed, there had been one attempt already. Could we ask the Lord to endanger his life? Time was running out and a decision had to be made. We had to know that we had done everything we could for our brother, so we sent a message to Jesus and then waited.

I moved around the house, tending to Lazarus restlessly but hopefully. I promised him that Jesus would soon be here and everything would be all right. How wrong I was! Jesus did not come and Lazarus did not recover.

I was puzzled—deeply disturbed, even—by the returning messengers' words. Jesus had said that Lazarus' sickness would not end in death—that all this was happening for the glory of God, so that the Son of God would receive glory. What could he mean? Mary and I sat beside our brother, watching him drift in and out of consciousness, hearing his breathing become increasingly shallow, until the last breath faded away.

I buried my brother with my sister at my side. I believed with all my heart that Jesus was the Chosen One, the Son of God, and the death of my brother did not change that, but why had Jesus said these words and why had he stayed away? While these questions troubled me on one level, I had an extraordinary sense of peace that carried me through the dreadful days of death, burial and mourning. Perhaps it was due to my strong belief in the final resurrection, when we would see Lazarus again, or perhaps the peace was God-given. Oh, I wept, but below the tears was something—or someone—holding me.

I was glad of the household duties that could occupy some of those long days following Lazarus' death; they gave me momentary distraction from the pain within. I craved to be occupied with some menial task.

When the message came that Jesus was outside the village, I jumped up straight away and took Mary's arm, but she looked up at me through her tear-filled eyes and shook her head. So I went alone to meet him. I walked swiftly, my hope growing with every step I took. Perhaps it wasn't too late, after all.

As soon as I reached Jesus, my pain and hope found voice: 'Lord, if only you had been here, my brother would not have died. But even now, I know that God will give you whatever you ask.'[29] I wanted Jesus to know that I still believed in him.

'Lazarus will rise again,' Jesus replied.

'Yes, I know. He will rise when we all do on that last day.' Was this not the hope that had comforted me through these dark days?

'I am the resurrection and the life. Anyone who believes in me will live, even after dying. Everyone who lives in me and believes in me will never die. Do you believe this, Martha?'[30]

I felt a burning in my heart as Jesus uttered these words. Faith, hope and love welled up within me. 'Yes, Lord. I have always believed since I first met you that you are the Messiah, the Son of God, the one who has come into the world from God.'

'Where is Mary?' Jesus asked. 'I dearly want to see her.'

I knew that I must get back to Mary and persuade her to come. I wanted to tell her what Jesus had said, to give her hope. I hurried back as fast as I could and asked a mourner to bring Mary to me. The moment I said that the teacher was asking for her, she left. I had no opportunity to tell her of the wonderful conversation that I had had with Jesus.

I will leave Mary to tell you what happened next.

Reflection and discussion

- Did any words or phrases stand out for you? Before further discussion, read the rest or all of the passage again in a different translation or paraphrase of the Bible.

- In the monologue, Mary and Martha work together to care for their brother in his sickness, finding a unity in shared purpose. Our country's history and our personal histories reveal that there are times when differences are buried because of a common objective, when people discover a unity of heart and mind. How can we keep our focus on Christ and foster unity in church life?

- One of the final prayers of Jesus was for the unity of his followers. Read John 17:20–21: 'I am praying not only for these disciples but also for all who will ever believe in me through their message. I pray that they will all be one, just as you and I are one—as you are in me, Father, and I am in you. And may they be in us so that the world will believe you sent me.' However, biblical and church history, as well as our own experience of church, shows that unity does not always seem to be possible. This can leave us scarred. Share ways in which we can recover from such experiences.

- In this episode Martha's belief in Jesus shines through her grief: 'Even now I know that God will give you whatever you ask... I have always believed you are the Messiah, the Son of God, the one who has come into the world from God' (John 11:22, 27). We see people who are suffering greatly amid personal tragedy, who do not witness the fulfilment of promises or consider their prayers answered and yet still hang onto their faith. Share examples that you have come across. How can we emulate this quality of faith?

■ We sometimes experience a deep peace that we cannot logically explain in the midst of a crisis. Share times when you have known this peace for yourself or observed it in others. Read the following verses together and make time during the week to meditate on them. 'The eternal God is your refuge, and underneath are the everlasting arms' (Deuteronomy 33:27, NIV). 'You will keep in perfect peace those whose minds are steadfast, because they trust in you' (Isaiah 26:3, NIV). 'And the peace of God, which transcends all understanding, will guard your hearts and your minds in Christ Jesus' (Philippians 4:7, NIV).

■ In these monologues the reactions of Mary and Martha to the death of Lazarus are very different. Reactions to the death of a loved one are individual: some bereaved people prefer to be occupied and others have little energy available with which to do anything. We need to respect and understand both these reactions. In what practical ways can we support people in their diverse responses?

■ This passage was referred to in the previous study on Martha, in which Martha's honesty with Jesus and deep faith in her Lord were noted. The episode is also full of hope. With faith in Christ, the 'sting of death' is taken away. We can hold on to the words of Jesus: 'I am the resurrection and the life. Anyone who believes in me will live, even after dying. Everyone who lives in me and believes in me will never ever die' (John 11:25–26).

■ Hope is a biblical quality that we are to seek to develop in our lives. In Paul's well-known chapter on love, we find the conclusion, 'Three things will last forever—faith, hope, and love—and the greatest of these is love' (1 Corinthians 13:13). How do faith, hope and love sustain us amidst difficult circumstances?

- Read together these verses on hope and find the opportunity to meditate on them when alone: 'And we rejoice in the hope of the glory of God. Not only so, but we also rejoice in our sufferings, because we know that suffering produces perseverance; perseverance, character; and character, hope. And hope does not disappoint us, because God has poured out his love into our hearts by the Holy Spirit, whom he has given us' (Romans 5:2–5, NIV). 'We who have fled to him for refuge can have great confidence as we hold to the hope that lies before us. This hope is a strong and trustworthy anchor for our souls' (Hebrews 6:18–19). Share times when hope has been an 'anchor for your soul'.

- How has reflecting on this episode deepened your faith in Jesus, Son of God?

Conclusion

Take time to pray through your findings. What might God be saying to you? Is anything particularly relevant to your life at the moment? Write down what you have learnt and refer back to it regularly in the days ahead so that it becomes part of your thinking, reacting and lifestyle.

Jesus and Mary at the raising of Lazarus (Part 2)

Introduction

- Read John 11:1–46. You may like to read the first 16 verses before the monologue and the rest of the verses after it.

- Ask God to speak to you through this episode. You could use the words from Psalm 119:17: 'Bless me with life so that I can continue to obey you' (LB).

- Sit back, relax and close your eyes. Imagine the scene as someone reads out the monologue.

Monologue

It had all happened so suddenly. One moment Lazarus, my dearly loved brother, was fine, and the next he was seriously ill. To start with, I had not worried unduly, for he was a strong man and a capable provider for us. Martha and I did all we could to help him and I was sure he would recover, but he got worse so quickly. Watching someone you love suffer like that, while being unable to make a difference, is dreadful. But of course, we knew someone who could make a difference—Jesus. Had he not made the lame walk and the blind see, and even healed lepers?

We heard that Jesus had gone down to the River Jordan, so we sent messengers, expecting them to return with him. I waited eagerly but they returned alone, telling us that Jesus had said that Lazarus' sickness would not end in death. I think

Jesus' words would have filled us with hope if it was not for the evidence before our eyes, for Lazarus was struggling to breathe and was no longer eating or drinking. We knew death was near.

Lazarus did not live to see the next day dawn, yet hadn't Jesus said that our brother would live? Into my heart crept a seed of doubt that gnawed away at my soul whenever there was a quiet moment, slowly undermining my trust in Jesus. Dazed, I accepted our grieving friends and relatives from Bethany and Jerusalem into the house, their tears mingling with mine. We did all that the law required and Lazarus was bound in cloth and laid in the tomb.

I felt I had lost two friends and brothers, for had not Lazarus and Jesus been friends and brothers to me? One had left me through death and the other had not come when I most needed him. So I grieved a double loss.

Four days later, a message came to the house that Jesus was approaching. Martha immediately got up and left to meet him. I did not, for it was all too late. The irony of his coming now caused me to weep anew and my comforters clustered around me.

I remember a gentle tapping on my shoulder, and a mourner pointed out Martha to me. She had returned with a message. 'The teacher is here and wants to see you,' she whispered.

I went immediately, hurrying, stumbling along the streets to the edge of the village, my vision blurred by tears. Why did I go now when earlier I had stayed in the house? I had a question to ask him—one that needed answering. I was aware of footsteps behind me and turned briefly to see that my comforters had followed me. No doubt they thought that I was going back to the tomb.

Then I saw Jesus; he was standing just beyond the first of the village houses. I ran and fell at his feet, and my question, the question, 'Why did you not come when I needed you?' came out as a statement: 'Lord, if only you had been here, my brother would not have died.'

There was no reply and the silence was filled with my weeping and the wailing of those who had now caught up with me. At last I looked up at Jesus. I am not sure what I expected to see on his face, but what I found shook me to the core. I saw distress but also anger, raging anger. Not anger directed at me, though. In Jesus' anger I recognised my own anger—seething rage that a man as needed and loved as my brother could be snatched away by death; fury that this world is so marred. Deeply troubled, he turned to the gathering crowd. 'Where have you put him?' he asked.

'Come and see, Lord,' was the reply.

Jesus wept. At that moment I knew that my Lord shared my grief. My doubts about his love for my family disappeared. I still did not know why he had not come to us, but I did know that he cared. His tears were my tears—tears of anger and sadness.

So we stood apart from the crowd, Jesus and me. I could overhear their words, though. Some marvelled, 'See how much he loved Lazarus.' Others muttered with the mutterings of my own heart, 'This man has healed blind men. Could he not have stopped Lazarus from dying?'

Jesus' tears stopped flowing but I could still sense his anger as we made our way to the tomb, feel the anger in his body as he walked purposefully towards it. There it was, Lazarus' burial place, with the large stone rolled across its entrance.

'Roll the stone aside,' Jesus ordered.

A gasp went up from the crowd. I looked up at Jesus in astonishment and my sister protested gently, 'Lord, we can't do that. He has been dead four days.' But Jesus looked resolute.

'Lord, there will be a terrible smell,' Martha tried to persuade him. The very thought of my brother's decaying body sickened me. Was it not bad enough that Jesus had stayed away when he was most needed? Now he was intending to put us through the agony of seeing the dead body.

Jesus, addressing the disciples who had come with him and the mourners, said, 'Did I not tell you that you would see God's glory if you believe?' So they did it. Young, strong men from the crowd stepped forward and started to push the stone—men who followed Jesus wherever he went, who were prepared to do whatever he said, even open the tomb of a dead man.

The crowd was silent, many retreating, horrified at the outrage taking place before them. I stood transfixed, staring at the gaping hole.

Jesus stepped forward, looked up to heaven and said in a voice for all to hear, 'Father, thank you for hearing me. I know that you always hear me, but for the sake of those around me I say these words aloud. As a result of this, may they believe that you sent me!'

With a loud shout that echoed in and out of the cave, Jesus called, 'Lazarus, come out!'

Utter silence followed. Then, those of us who were near enough heard a slight noise from within the tomb. No one moved. Every eye was focused on that dark hole. Unmistakably, the sound of shuffling was getting nearer, and then... there was Lazarus in the entrance, his arms and legs bound in graveclothes, his face wrapped in a headcloth.

Still no one moved—no one apart from Jesus. Turning to face us, he said, with a look of joy on his face, 'Well, unwrap him, then. Let him go!'

What celebrations we had! What laughter we shared together once again in our home with Jesus! Many believed in Jesus that day. But some, in spite of the miracle they had witnessed, did not believe. In fact, they betrayed Jesus to the Pharisees by telling them what Jesus had done.

Reflection and discussion

- Did any words or phrases stand out for you? Before further discussion, read the rest or all of the passage again in a different translation or paraphrase of the Bible.

- Mary felt that Jesus had not been there for her when she needed him; she was probably aware that he was performing miracles in other people's lives while she was left feeling abandoned. Do you have times when God does not seem to be there for you, perhaps when you can see him working in other people's lives while areas of your own life are going from bad to worse? Perhaps there are times when your prayers seem to go unanswered and you are puzzled by the apparent silence of God. There may have been times when his words and promises did not ring true with your life experiences. Share some of these times, if you feel able. Expressing such feelings to others can prevent resentment and bitterness from building up and can help us on our spiritual journey.

- What value can you see in the 'wilderness' experience, the time when God seems silent? In our darkest times, God is still with us: 'In a desert land he found him, in a barren and howling waste. He shielded him and cared for him; he guarded him as the apple of his eye' (Deuteronomy 32:10, NIV).

- We sometimes withdraw from God when times are hard: in this episode, initially Mary did not go with Martha to Jesus. He then asked for Mary, ready to comfort her, but it was her choice as to whether or not she would respond to his invitation. Share times when you have withdrawn from the Lord, either consciously or unconsciously, and say what brought you back to him.

- Notice the honesty of Mary's words to Jesus: 'Lord, if only you had been here, my brother would not have died' (John 11:32). How honest are your prayers? Mary dared to be open, even in front of other people. What can we learn from this?

- We may not understand what is happening to us or God's actions or lack of actions, but realising that God does care and feels our grief with intensity can soothe our troubled minds. 'Yet it was our weaknesses he carried; it was our sorrows that weighed him down... He was beaten so we could be whole. He was whipped so we could be healed' (Isaiah 53:4–5).

- In Romans 12:15 we read the words, 'Be happy with those who are happy, and weep with those who weep.' We see these words lived out by Jesus: he celebrated with friends at the wedding in Cana and he wept with Mary at the death of Lazarus. How easy is it to follow his example? If you are able, share occasions when you have done this, when it has proved helpful to the one with whom you have been grieving or rejoicing.

- In this episode Jesus expresses strong emotions of grief and anger: 'A deep anger welled up within him… Then Jesus wept… Jesus was still angry as he arrived at the tomb' (John 11:33, 35, 38). Jesus' anger was also seen when he overturned the tables in the temple, and his grief when he considered the plight of Jerusalem. Are we familiar with this Jesus of strong passion, or do we see Jesus as 'meek and mild'? Appropriate emotions are a gift from God. How comfortable and able are we to express them?

- Jesus instructed the mourners to move the stone away. Would we be prepared to do something 'strange' for Jesus, something that defies logic? Share experiences you have had of doing this or of times when you felt unable to rise to the challenge.

- Jesus then instructs the mourners, 'Unwrap him and let him go!' (v. 44). We, like Lazarus, may have walked towards the light, to the edge of the tomb, but how far have we let God, through the love and support of others, 'unwrap' all that would prevent us from celebrating the freedom that Christ has given us? Think about this when you are reflecting at the end of the session.

- It is hard to comprehend that some people still did not believe in spite of this miracle, but Jesus says in Luke 16:31, 'If they do not listen to Moses and the Prophets, they will not be convinced even if someone rises from the dead' (NIV). We can share God's love through word and action, but are not responsible for the response of others. The journey to faith is the responsibility of the individual. How can this knowledge release us from pressure?

- How have Jesus words and actions in this episode enabled you to know him better?

Conclusion

Take time to pray through your findings. What might God be saying to you? Is anything particularly relevant to your life at the moment? Write down what you have learnt and refer back to it regularly in the days ahead so that it becomes part of your thinking, reacting and lifestyle.

Jesus anointed at Bethany by Mary

Introduction

- Read John 12:1–8.

- Ask God to speak to you through this episode. You could use the words from Psalm 119:117: 'Sustain me, and I will be rescued; then I will meditate continually on your decrees.'

- Sit back, relax and close your eyes. Imagine the scene as someone reads out the monologue.

Monologue

Once again Jesus was in our home, but that night was different. The house was packed with people who had heard about my brother, Lazarus, whom Jesus raised from the dead. They had been awaiting their opportunity to meet Jesus for themselves. Martha and I were to be found in our usual places: Martha was preparing food and I was sitting at the feet of Jesus. This time, however, there was a difference: we were both at ease with ourselves, each with our own way of expressing love for him.

There was another difference, too—the atmosphere. Gone were our euphoria and excitement, for we had heard enough rumours of plots to kill Jesus to know that he was in great danger. It had been a while since he had appeared in public; we had understood that he was out in the wilderness, teaching the disciples in quiet safety. But with Passover approaching, people were wondering whether he would attend the celebrations and come in time for the purification ceremony.

Then Jesus and his disciples had arrived at our house, with just six days to go before the feast. I quaked at the thought that perhaps someone in this very room would betray my dearest friend to the authorities. I knew with a sudden certainty that this precious time with my Lord was coming to an end, and a suffocating grief filled my soul. How could I just sit here when I sensed what was ahead? What could I say to let him know that I understood and that I loved him with all my heart? There was nothing I could say, but perhaps there was something I could do.

I crept quietly from the group encircling him and returned with a jar of ointment held secretively in the folds of my dress. It contained nard, an extremely expensive perfume, and it was the most valuable treasure I possessed. Working my way back to sit at Jesus' feet was not difficult, for it was where the disciples expected to see me. Once there, I removed the jar and started to pour the ointment over his feet.

As the perfume rose through the house, a deathly hush descended. I sensed the eyes of everyone boring into my back. The words Jesus was speaking slowly faded as he looked down at me, watching me tenderly. The perfume ran over his feet but I had no cloth to dry them. So I undid my hair, letting it fall down to my waist. Some of the men gasped at my audacity in loosening my hair in public. I bent over and started to wipe up the excess perfume with it.

The silence was cut in two by the words of Judas Iscariot, the disciple who looked after the disciples' money. 'That perfume is worth a year's wages. It should have been sold and then we could have given the money to the poor,' he growled.

Once again my behaviour had led to criticism. Would my

Lord agree with him or would I find understanding, even approval, as I had when Martha had criticised me?

His reply affirmed me but filled my heart with fear for his future. 'Leave her alone. She did this in preparation for my burial. You will always have the poor among you, but you will not always have me.'[31]

I stood, my vision blurred by tears at his words. The rest of that evening was tense and strained, with little conversation. We were absorbed in our fears and anxieties, which were turning to a dreadful apprehension of what might lie ahead for our Lord.

Reflection and discussion

- Did any words or phrases stand out for you? Before further discussion, read the passage again in a different translation or paraphrase of the Bible.

- In this monologue, Mary and Martha are at peace, accepting that they each have a different way of expressing their love for Jesus. The five languages to express love are described as the giving of gifts, acts of service, giving time, giving words and giving touch.[32] We see Martha loving Jesus through acts of service and words (John 11:27), and Mary loving him through the giving of a precious gift, spending time with him, and touch. Spend time discussing your most natural 'love languages'. How do they apply to your relationship with God? Which of the 'love languages' would you like to develop in your relationship with God?

- It can be easy to criticise or to be embarrassed by the extravagant displays of love that others may show God. Share any experiences you have had of this. What can we learn from this passage?

- On the surface, there can seem to be a discrepancy between the instruction that Jesus gave to the rich religious leader in Luke 18:18–25 and the words of Jesus in this episode. Read the verses and discuss this issue. There may be times on our spiritual journey when we are challenged, either by the needs of others or by our love for the Lord, to generous acts of giving. We are called to provide for our families but also to care for the poor and vulnerable. We need to work out how best to do this, knowing that, in reality, in this fallen world we will always have the poor among us. Some people find that it is more meaningful to support an individual child, a specific family or project. Share your thoughts.

- Loving Jesus brought Mary criticism. This can happen in many different ways. Share your experiences of the criticisms or conflicts that loving Jesus can bring. Encourage each other.

- What do we learn of Jesus in this study? His wholehearted acceptance of the love and worship that Mary showed can encourage us in our faltering steps to know and worship him.

Conclusion

Take time to pray through your findings. What might God be saying to you? Is anything particularly relevant to your life at the moment? Write down what you have learnt and refer back to it regularly in the days ahead so that it becomes part of your thinking, reacting and lifestyle.

Jesus watches the widow give all that she has

Introduction

- Read Luke 21:1–4.

- Ask God to speak to you through this episode. You could use the words from Psalm 119:149: 'In your faithful love, O Lord, hear my cry; let me be revived by following your regulations.'

- Sit back, relax and close your eyes. Imagine the scene as someone reads out the monologue.

Monologue

It was all I had left, those two small coins. There was no way—or, I should say, no moral way—to earn my keep: my husband was dead and I had no grown sons to provide for me.

Although it was a while since his death, I still found myself thinking in each situation, 'What would my husband have done?' He had been so devout, with such a love for God and desire to keep his commands. He would have given God a tenth, a tithe. The only difficulty was that you could not tithe such a tiny amount. I would either have to give all of it or half of it.

I tried to keep myself from the waves of panic that flooded over me by focusing on the stories that my mother had told me, the stories that my husband and I had discussed so often. I thought of the widow of Zarephath who was instructed by God to feed the prophet Elijah. There was one problem: she had almost no food herself. In fact, she was collecting sticks to make a fire on which to cook a final loaf for herself and her son when Elijah met her. She did not expect to survive, but Elijah told her that if she made him a loaf from the small amount of flour and oil she had left, the flour and oil would never run out. They would last until the famine was over.

It happened exactly as he had said. What relief and joy they must have known! But how much courage had it taken to give away that precious bread? Did the containers look empty as she poured their contents out and made that 'final' loaf? At what point did she know that there was more left for herself and her son? Perhaps it was not until she next needed a meal. Could I have done that?

Then I thought of the widow who had nothing left but a flask of olive oil and turned to the prophet of God, Elisha, for help. He instructed her to fill all the jars she could find with the oil. It flowed and flowed until the containers were full. With all that oil to sell, how they must have laughed and celebrated!

Really it was obvious what I had to do. Like the widow of Zarephath, I had to give all that I had without knowing for sure that I would survive. I had to trust God even though life had dealt me so many blows that I barely knew what the word 'trust' meant any more.

I set off for the temple and, as I climbed the steps, I overheard excited yet nervous whispers: 'He's here!' I knew who 'he' was—Jesus! Many people thought he was the last prophet; some even thought he was our long-awaited Messiah. I had heard of his miracles and teaching and wondered what my husband would have made of him. What did I make of him? I wasn't sure.

Once in the temple, I joined the queue of people giving their money, clutching my two coins in embarrassment as I saw others parting with large amounts. When my turn came, I dropped the coins in with my head held low and my eyes filled with tears of despair.

It was done; I turned to hurry away, only to find myself face to face with the prophet, Jesus. It was as if he were there waiting for me. He smiled such a smile of reassurance that my heart dared to hope. This prophet had come to rescue me, just as had happened in times of old.

Turning to his disciples, Jesus spoke these words of affirmation that I will always remember: 'The truth is that this widow has given more money than all the rest of them. You see, they gave a part of what they had spare and yet she, the poorest, gave all she had.'

My Elijah, my Elisha, had come to rescue me.

Reflection and discussion

■ Did any words or phrases stand out for you? Before further discussion, read the passage again in a different translation or paraphrase of the Bible.

■ We do not know what happened next, but we can be sure that there was provision for the widow. Did the disciples supply her needs from their 'kitty'? Did Jesus place her into the safe keeping of a follower, as he did his own mother when he asked John to care for her? We can only imagine.

■ One of the names for God in the Old Testament is Jehovah Jirah, which means 'God my Provider'. God promises to meet our needs, not our wants. Read Philippians 4:19: 'And my God will meet all your needs according to his glorious riches in Christ Jesus.' (NIV 1984). This provision is not limited to material things; also, the provision may or may not seem miraculous. Encourage each other by sharing ways in which you have experienced God's provision, be it material, emotional or spiritual. Sometimes it can seem as if provision is withheld until the last minute. Discuss reasons why this might be.

- In the monologue, the widow is portrayed as being on a spiritual journey; she is a devout believer in God but is still on her way to understanding who Jesus is. Jesus affirms her 'where she is', which moves her on in her journey. Imagine how her journey would have been set back if she had met with ridicule or criticism from one of the disciples. We have the same opportunity to help others move on in their journey. Sometimes the journey is very slow and sometimes quick. Share your experiences of occasions when you know you have stepped forward or backward in your journey with God. What caused this movement?

- We have imagined that the widow will always remember the words of Jesus. It is easy for us to hear from God, be excited about it and then fail to remember or put into practice the revelation we have had. The Bible compares this experience to looking in a mirror and then forgetting what we have seen (James 1:22–24). What practical measures can we take to prevent this and to ensure that our spiritual journey continues? In the conclusion for each of these studies, we are encouraged to write down and pray through what God might be saying to us, particularly anything that is relevant to our lives at the moment, referring back to our notes in the days ahead. This is the beginning of keeping a spiritual journal. Such a journal can be written daily, weekly or less frequently. It provides a private record of our walk with God and enables us to reflect on our lives, while the act of writing helps to clarify our thinking.

- The widow felt inferior when she saw other people's gifts. We too can struggle with feelings of inferiority when we see the abilities of others. In this passage, Jesus shows us that he values what we contribute. Share your experiences of these feelings.

- What draws you to Jesus in this study?

Conclusion

Take time to pray through your findings. What might God be saying to you? Is anything particularly relevant to your life at the moment? Write down what you have learnt and refer back to it regularly in the days ahead so that it becomes part of your thinking, reacting and lifestyle.

Mary's journey of suffering (Part 1)

The next two studies follow the suffering of Mary. If the monologues are being used as a read meditation without the studies, they can be used together, forming one continuous passage of prose.

Introduction

- Read Luke 4:14–30; 8:1–3; Matthew 12:46–50 and 13:53–58. Some of these passages could be read before the monologue and some of them afterwards.

- Ask God to speak to you through this episode. You could use the words from Psalm 119:116: 'Lord, sustain me as you promised, that I may live! Do not let my hope be crushed.'

- Sit back, relax and close your eyes. Imagine the scene as someone reads out the monologue.

Monologue

My 'yes' to God all those years ago, when the angel Gabriel visited me, had been voiced with an innocence that knew nothing of what would lie ahead for my son, Jesus, or of the suffering that he and I would endure.

I realise now that there were glimpses of rejection all along the way for both of us, from our escape into Egypt right up until that final rejection of my son by his people at Golgotha. Indeed, I believed that God himself had rejected us when I heard my son cry from the cross, 'My God, my God, why have you forsaken me?'[33]

News often reached my family from the nearby towns and villages where Jesus had been healing the sick and preaching about the kingdom of God. We heard that he had even raised the dead. In those days my heart was full of hope and anticipation; at last my son was revealing himself as the Messiah, the one my people had awaited.

I was unable to travel with Jesus but I knew that other women accompanied him and his disciples, supporting and resourcing their work. Some of these women had been cured of evil spirits and diseases. I was to get to know them in the dark days to come.

At last an opportunity came for me to go with my sons to hear Jesus speak and to spend some time with him. But when we arrived, the crowd was enormous and Jesus seemed so far away. We strained to catch his words. I longed to be with him. Attempting to move nearer, we found that any gaps in front of us closed rapidly. No one intended to give up a place.

Disappointed and tired after the journey, I asked if a message could be passed forward until it reached Jesus, to let him know that his family were there and wanted to see him. Perhaps my son would call us forward or even stop for a while and come and speak with us. But his response to our message not only took me by surprise; it hurt me deeply. There was a long pause and then Jesus said with a loud voice, 'Who is my mother? Who are my brothers?'

Then he pointed at those who travelled with him and said, 'Look, these are my mother and brothers. Anyone who does the will of my Father in heaven is my brother and sister and mother!'[34]

In the following days, as I recovered from the emotional

pain of the event, I came to be glad that my son had such a band of loyal and committed friends, whom he could regard as family. I glimpsed the big picture, which one glorious day I was to grasp fully: the kingdom of God was becoming established on earth, and a new way of relating to others in love was becoming possible.

I remember the time when we heard that Jesus was returning to Nazareth to preach in our synagogue. Already, reports praising my son were travelling around Galilee: he taught with such authority; he performed miracles. My excitement and hopes grew: the people among whom Jesus had grown up would finally realise who he was—the Chosen One of Israel. All my years of silence would be over. How I enjoyed having Jesus among us again. How I looked forward to the sabbath when I would hear him teach.

I sat in the synagogue with bated breath that sabbath. Surely the time had come. I watched as Jesus stood to read the scriptures, as he was handed a scroll, as he unrolled it and appeared to be finding a certain passage. Then he read, 'The Spirit of the Lord is upon me, for he has anointed me to bring Good News to the poor. He has sent me to proclaim that captives will be released, that the blind will see, that the oppressed will be set free, and that the time of the Lord's favour has come.'[35]

Slowly he rolled up the scroll, handed it back to the attendant and sat down. Not a sound was to be heard; every eye was fixed on Jesus, awaiting his words. Then came the words I had been longing to hear: 'The Scripture you've just heard has been fulfilled this very day!'[36]

How graciously my son spoke, for had we not heard that he had set free captives to evil spirits? Had not the blind man seen? I sensed those around me marvelling at his words, that the son of Joseph the carpenter could speak with such authority. I heard them wonder from where Jesus got his wisdom and the power to perform miracles.

Then something in the atmosphere started to change, subtly at first. The wonder started to turn to cynicism. The first words of scoffing cut my heart: 'He's just the carpenter's son, and we know Mary, his mother, and his brothers—James, Joseph, Simon and Judas. All his sisters live right here among us. Where did he learn all these things?'[37]

I wanted to get up, to tell them the secrets that I had long kept hidden, but I was helpless. How I longed to protect my son, but I could do nothing but listen as Jesus replied to the taunts: 'You will undoubtedly quote me this proverb: "Physician, heal yourself"—meaning, "Do miracles here in your home town like those you did in Capernaum." But I tell you the truth, no prophet is accepted in his own home town.'[38]

He argued his case from our Jewish history: 'Certainly there were many needy widows in Israel in Elijah's time, when the heavens were closed for three and a half years, and a severe famine devastated the land. Yet Elijah was not sent to any of them. He was sent instead to a foreigner—a widow of Zarephath in the land of Sidon. And there were many lepers in Israel in the time of the prophet Elisha, but the only one healed was Naaman, a Syrian.'[39]

My son had known, then, that this would be the case for him also. In his wisdom he had known that he would be rejected and would be able to perform only a few miracles here in his home town. Yet he had stood before them, ready to accept their taunts, wanting the people of Nazareth to have the opportunity to recognise him for who he was, the Son whom God had lovingly sent into the world.

The cynicism and scoffing started to become more hostile. I could see deep offence and fury in the eyes of the local men as they realised the implications of Jesus' words. They jumped up, forcing Jesus out of the synagogue, a crowd of them pushing him along the road to the edge of the hill on which Nazareth was built. I ran along beside them, ignoring hostile glances, breathless with anxiety as we approached the cliff. My son's life was in danger again and this time I could not save him.

'Listen to my cry for help!'[40] I called to God. Then, quite suddenly, there was silence. It was as if a presence surrounded Jesus, and the violent mob drew back. Jesus turned, walking right back through the middle of the crowd, and left.

Reflection and discussion

- Did any words or phrases stand out for you? Before further discussion, read some or all of the passages again in a different translation or paraphrase of the Bible.

- We can imagine the hurt and rejection that Mary may have felt when she heard the words of Jesus, 'These are my mother and brothers. Anyone who does the will of my Father in heaven is my brother and sister and mother' (Matthew 12:49–50). What do you make of this episode? It is clear that Jesus felt a huge sense of responsibility towards his mother and loved her dearly, because of his words on the cross in which he makes provision for her through his disciple, John. Rather than being negative about his own family, in this statement Jesus was indicating the depth of spiritual friendship and commitment that is possible between believers. The community of believers is a spiritual family. Have you experienced this? How can we move towards this ideal in our busy and often fractured lives?

- Like Mary, sometimes we are not able to support directly those we love, but have to prayerfully leave them in the hands of others and God. Can you share examples of this from your life? How easy or difficult was it?

- In the monologue, Mary is imagined to recover from this episode as she glimpses the big picture: 'the kingdom of God was becoming established on earth, and a new way of relating to others in love was becoming possible.' We can get so involved in the details of life that we lose the big picture. If we can keep our perspective, we may be able to react less negatively to the events that absorb our emotional energy. Share times when looking at the bigger picture has helped you.

- Jesus' words, 'No prophet is accepted in his own home town', show that he was expecting rejection in Nazareth. Yet he came to the place of his upbringing, announcing in a very public way that he was the fulfilment of Isaiah's prophecy, giving everyone the occasion to respond. Jesus does not force himself upon us but gives opportunities to us to come to faith: 'He doesn't want anyone lost. He's giving everyone space and time to change' (2 Peter 3:9, THE MESSAGE). Jesus longed for his people to respond to him. To the people of Jerusalem he spoke the words, 'How often I have wanted to gather your children together as a hen protects her chicks beneath her wings, but you wouldn't let me' (Matthew 23:37). Share with one another the gentle and loving ways in which Jesus has given you opportunities to respond to him and to grow in faith and understanding.

- There is a challenge in this episode as we recognise in the attitudes of the Nazarenes our own tendency to cynicism. When other believers talk of a faith-life beyond our experience or comfort zone, do we inwardly or even outwardly respond with cynicism? When we see someone younger than us—perhaps someone we have known as a child—speak out powerfully in God's name, do we experience some discomfort or cynicism? Have we ever listened to a preacher with cynicism? Cynicism is not the same as shrewdness, which Jesus advocates: 'Therefore be as shrewd as snakes and as innocent as doves' (Matthew 10:16, NIV). How can we be spiritually shrewd without being cynical?

- In the monologue, Mary is imagined to cry out to God, 'Listen to my cry for help' from Psalm 5:2. The psalms can be very helpful in prayer, containing words that reflect the spectrum of human experience and emotion. Share with each other times when a particular psalm has been meaningful to you.

- Short cries to God for help, as Mary is imagined to have prayed, are sometimes called 'arrow prayers'. This expression was coined by Augustine of Hippo (Letter 130). They are often part of our daily walk with God, and there may be some that we frequently 'shoot' up to heaven. Share some of your arrow prayers. Take encouragement from the knowledge that God is 'our refuge and strength, an ever-present help in trouble' (Psalm 46:1, NIV).

Conclusion

Take time to pray through your findings. What might God be saying to you? Is anything particularly relevant to your life at the moment? Write down what you have learnt and refer back to it regularly in the days ahead so that it becomes part of your thinking, reacting and lifestyle.

Mary's journey of suffering (Part 2)

Introduction

- Read John 7:1–9; 12:12–15; 19:1–6; Luke 23:26–28 and John 19:23–30. Some of these passages could be read before the monologue and some of them afterwards. In your own time you could also look at Matthew 27:27–56; Mark 15:21–41 and Luke 23:29–49.

- Ask God to speak to you through this episode. You could use the words from Psalm 119:76: 'Now let your unfailing love comfort me, just as you promised me, your servant.'

- Sit back, relax and close your eyes. Imagine the scene as someone reads out the monologue.

Monologue

Since Jesus was rejected in Nazareth, the words he had spoken gnawed at my heart: 'A prophet is honoured everywhere except... among his own family.'[41] I was aware of the feelings among my other sons, of their growing disbelief in Jesus and their suspicion that he was mad,[42] and this caused me great suffering. My anxiety for Jesus' well-being was growing daily, for we heard that Jews in Judea were waiting to take his life. So Jesus was spending more time in Galilee. My sons' impatience with Jesus grew until, as we neared the time of the feast of Tabernacles, they started to ridicule him, trying to persuade him to go up to Jerusalem for the celebrations, to make himself known by performing miracles there.

I could hear the mockery in their voices as they said, 'No one who wants to become a public figure acts in secret. Since you are doing these things, show yourself to the world.'[43] I grieved this lack of unity within my family. But Jesus told his brothers to go to the feast without him, for 'the time was not yet right for him'. I pondered on what these words could mean.

'The world hates me because I accuse it of doing evil,' Jesus said. His words frightened me and left me utterly bewildered. Had the angel not said that God would give his Son the throne of David, that he would rule over Israel for ever and that his kingdom would never end? Yet, although many people flocked to him, he was being rejected by our leaders; their hostility was turning to hatred. How could these promises ever be fulfilled?

I had enjoyed 30 years watching my son turn from boy to man. These last three years, although often far from him and anxious for him, I had rejoiced in his teaching and the miracles that he brought into the lives of others. But that Passover week in a heaving Jerusalem was agony beyond comparison.

I was there with him all the way to the cross.

I was there when the crowds welcomed Jesus into Jerusalem, throwing their cloaks before the colt he rode. I heard their shouts of 'Hosanna to the King of Israel.'

I was there when the same crowds shouted, 'Crucify him!'

I saw Jesus standing before Pilate, a purple robe around his shoulders and a crown of thorns on his head, his body bruised from flogging, blood running down his face.

I was there when my son fell from the weight of carrying the cross. I saw the soldiers force a passing man to carry it.

I was there when they took his clothes. I watched the soldiers gamble for them.

I was there when they crucified my firstborn. I stood near the cross. I met his eyes. I heard his final words to me, 'Dear woman, here is your son,' and his final words to John, 'Here is your mother.'

I heard the cruel taunts. I heard Jesus forgive.

I heard my son welcome a thief into Paradise.

I stood in the darkness as my son called out to God in his abandonment and then entrusted himself to his Father.

I was there when my son cried out in thirst.

I was there as he uttered the words, 'It is finished.'

I saw his head fall forwards. And my heart was broken.

Reflection and discussion

- Did any words or phrases stand out for you? Before further discussion, read some or all of the passages again in a different translation or paraphrase of the Bible.

- Mary had to live with the pain of knowing that her other sons did not believe in Jesus. It can be very painful to have a faith that is not shared by those closest to you. It may be that you are surrounded by unbelievers or that your children have grown up to reject your faith, or it may be that members of your family, although believers, are uncomfortable with the way in which you express your faith. Share your experiences and commit to supporting one another through friendship and prayer.

- Jesus' brothers had difficulty believing in him. Do you sympathise with them? His way of life was so very different from the one that, as Jewish men, they would have expected of the Messiah. They finally believed after the evidence of

Jesus' death and resurrection: his brother, James, became one of the leaders of the early church. In Acts 1:14 we read that after the ascension of Jesus, his mother Mary and his brothers, as well as several other women, were among the followers who 'met together and were constantly united in prayer.' They would also have been present at Pentecost, for Acts 2:1 says that 'all the believers were meeting together in one place.'

- Mary's willingness to take a difficult path resulted in blessing for the whole world through Jesus. Although living through such pain, she was eventually to be 'blessed among women' as she came to understand the many things she had 'treasured in her heart', for she bore witness to the resurrected Christ, the ascension of Jesus and the coming of the Holy Spirit at Pentecost. Are there times of pain that you have been able to use for the blessing of others?

- Mary's 'yes' to God resulted in a journey that involved much suffering. This is the case for many people around the world. Take some time to pray for those who endure hardship because of their faith; pray that they will be comforted by the knowledge that 'what we suffer now is nothing compared to the glory he will reveal to us later' (Romans 8:18).

- Many Old Testament prophecies referred to details of the crucifixion and the events leading up to it. If time permits, you may want to look at the following: the entry into Jerusalem on a colt (Zechariah 9:9); casting lots for the clothing of Jesus (Psalm 22:18); the bones of Jesus left unbroken (Psalm 34:20); Jesus crucified alongside transgressors, pouring out his life to death (Isaiah 53:12); insults hurled at Jesus as he hung on the cross (Psalm 22:7); darkness falling on the land at noon (Amos 8:9). The detail of these prophecies demonstrates God's sovereign control over all the events surrounding the death of Jesus. How can this encourage us when world or personal circumstances threaten to overwhelm us?

■ What have you learnt of Jesus through this study?

Conclusion

Take time to pray through your findings. What might God be saying to you? Is anything particularly relevant to your life at the moment? Write down what you have learnt and refer back to it regularly in the days ahead so that it becomes part of your thinking, reacting and lifestyle.

Jesus and Mary Magdalene

Introduction

- Read Matthew 27:55–65; 28:1–10; Mark 16:1–11; Luke 23:49–55; 24:1–12; John 19:38–42 and 20:1–18. Some of these passages could be read before the monologue and some of them afterwards.

- Ask God to speak to you through this episode. You could use the words from Psalm 119:57–58: 'Lord, you are mine! I promise to obey your words! With all my heart I want your blessings. Be merciful as you promised.'

- Sit back, relax and close your eyes. Imagine the scene as someone reads out the monologue.

Monologue

That sabbath day passed so slowly, our forced inactivity making us captives to our thoughts. We women huddled together, going over the events of the previous day, our minds filled with harrowing images of our Lord and his suffering.

It had all been such a rush at the end. We heard that Joseph of Arimathea had been to Pilate to get permission to take our Lord's body. We watched, clinging to each other as we wept, as Joseph removed Jesus' lifeless body from the cross, wrapped him in spices and ointment and then wound linen around his body before taking it to a nearby garden, to a new tomb carved from rock. 'Why was a member of the Jewish high council performing such a risky act?' we wondered. All we could learn was that he was a godly man who was waiting for the kingdom of God to come; he had not supported the action of the other religious leaders.

Joseph was helped by Nicodemus, the religious leader who had come to speak to Jesus one night. Nicodemus, too, was putting his future in jeopardy.

We had followed them all the way to the garden tomb. Then Mary, mother of James and Joses, and I sat at a distance, watching Joseph place Jesus' body in the tomb before rolling a large stone across the entrance. That was the final moment of separation and I fell to the ground in grief. I felt the other women lift me from the dusty earth, telling me that we must hurry away, for the dabbath was upon us.

That sabbath day, we tried to take on board the enormity of what had happened. Our lives had been taken up with following our Lord and meeting his needs. Now we faced an unknown future. We felt a mounting anguish that we had not carried out those final rituals; we needed to know that we had done all we could for Jesus, and that included treating his body with love and respect. So our plan was made during those dreary, black hours. As soon as the sabbath was over we intended to buy further spices, return to the tomb and anoint Jesus' body.

We did not all have the courage to go through with this plan, but I went right to the tomb, as did Mary, the mother of James. We set out very early in the morning while it was still dark, clutching our spices. We were discussing who would roll the stone away for us when we heard a terrifying rumbling and the ground below us shook. From the direction of the garden we saw a bright light, so dazzling that we were forced to cover our eyes. Filled with terror, most of our group sank to the ground. We sat in silence, waiting for further tremors, but there was absolute stillness. Eventually I said that I wanted to continue, but only Mary was prepared to enter the garden with me.

We spoke not a word to each other as we walked on. The garden was an eerie place that morning, and yet the light was increasing with each moment, enabling us to retrace our steps to the tomb where we had seen Joseph place the body of Jesus. But when we arrived, what a sight met our eyes: the stone had already been rolled back. Perhaps there had been some sort of earthquake.

I looked towards the entrance and then questioningly at Mary. She nodded and I took her hand as, trembling, we moved slowly forward. Quietly we entered the tomb, our eyes adjusting to the dim light of the interior. I looked towards the stone slab where we had seen the body laid, but Jesus was not there. Desperately I glanced around the cave, for some illogical reason thinking that the body might be elsewhere in the tomb, but there was nothing. We looked at each other, completely bemused.

'Where is he?' I whispered. But before Mary had time to reply, two men in shining robes suddenly appeared. We fell to the ground petrified, hiding our faces in our hands.

'Do not be afraid. We know that you are looking for Jesus of Nazareth. Why are you looking among the dead for someone who is alive? He is not here. He has risen from the dead! Look, this is where they laid his body. Now, go and tell his disciples, including Peter, that Jesus is going ahead of you to Galilee. You will see him there, just as he told you before he died. Remember what he told you back in Galilee, that the Son of Man must be betrayed into the hands of sinful men and be crucified, and that he would rise again on the third day.'

Then I remembered all that Jesus had told us—those words that, at the time, had made no sense. Could it be? Could it possibly be that he was alive again? Like the widow's son, like Jairus' daughter, like our friend Lazarus? Hope rose slowly within me and I started to look up, but the angelic beings disappeared. I looked at Mary but saw no hope in her face, just complete bewilderment. Taking her arm, we stumbled out of the tomb and back into the early morning light to Joanna, Salome and the other women.

We breathlessly told them our story as we hurried to the house where the disciples had hidden themselves. I was brimming with excitement, wanting to believe with all my heart that Jesus was alive. We burst into the room. 'They have taken the Lord's body and we don't know where they have put him,' I said.

I told them about the angels, about my hope that perhaps no one had taken the body, that in some way that I could not understand, Jesus was alive again. I looked to Mary for confirmation of my story, and to the other women, but they were silent, full of fear.

As I looked at each of the disciples, I realised that they did not believe me, that I stood alone. They started to make allowances for me, telling me to sit down and rest, that I had been under too much strain, that I had imagined it, that I was talking nonsense, or that we had been to the wrong tomb. Oh, the excuses came, and I knew that they were remembering the old Mary of Magdala, the unstable hallucinating woman that I had been before I met Jesus. Did they no longer believe that Jesus had transformed me when he had cast out those demons? Did they no longer believe in him? Their words started to gnaw away at my confidence, at my hope, and I started to doubt myself. Had I imagined it?

Peter and John had not joined in with the other disciples but listened silently, watching me. Seeing my mounting distress, they said they would go to the tomb and look for themselves. I followed them but, the moment we left the house, Peter and John started to run and I was left far behind. Tired as I was, I hurried on after them in the direction of the garden. Then I saw Peter racing back towards me, but he didn't even stop when he reached me—barely gave me a glance.

Next, as I was entering the garden, John ran past me, asking if I had seen Peter. I nodded and pointed in the direction from which I had come. What was the expression on John's face? I could not make it out.

So this time I walked through the garden alone and my tears started to flow—tears of frustration because I had not been believed, tears of sadness because I felt so utterly abandoned, and tears of doubt. Had I imagined it? After all, the other women had not supported my story. Perhaps my hope really had been futile. My Lord's body had been moved, that was all. I did not know where he was. I could not anoint his body. I could not grieve properly. There was no place where I could feel near to him. Tears streamed down my face—tears of lost hope, of utter despair.

I bent over, leaning on the rock above the entrance to the tomb, and once again looked inside. There I saw two beings, one at the place where my Lord's head would have rested and one where his feet would have been. But I felt no fear or astonishment this time, perhaps because my grief and self-doubt were so intense that I was no longer sure that I could believe what I saw with my own eyes.

'Woman, why are you crying?' one of the angelic beings asked.

'Because they have taken away my Lord and I don't know where they have put him,' I sobbed.

I turned away; after all, perhaps I was simply hallucinating, speaking to thin air.

Then I noticed a man standing nearby. By now it was full daylight, so I assumed that it was the gardener coming to tend the garden. My eyes were swollen with crying and I squinted with the brightness of the sun, unable to look up into his face.

'Dear woman, why are you crying? Who are you looking for?' he asked. Perhaps he could help me. I stopped, hiding my tear-stained face from his scrutiny, and whispered, 'Sir, if you have taken him away, tell me where you have put him and I will go and get him.'

'Mary!'

He knew my name and I knew his voice. Turning round and falling at his feet, stretching out to touch the hem of his robe, I cried, 'Rabboni, my teacher!' It was my Jesus, my Lord! He was alive! He was here! He was with me!

The words that Jesus uttered are engraved on my heart, for I of all people was entrusted with taking this most important of messages to his disciples. 'Don't cling to me, for I have not yet ascended to the Father. But go and find my brothers and tell them that I am ascending to my Father and your Father, to my God and your God.'

He was gone and I was changed. Joy replaced despair; light replaced darkness; confidence replaced self-doubt; purpose replaced emptiness. I rushed back to the disciples and knocked frantically on the locked door, shouting that I had a message for them. As the door was opened I burst into the room and cried out, 'I HAVE SEEN THE LORD!'

Reflection and discussion

- Did any words or phrases stand out for you? Before further discussion, read the rest or all of the passage again in a different translation or paraphrase of the Bible.

- Joseph of Arimathea, a secret disciple, made a surprising entrance on the scene in asking to take down the body of Jesus from the cross. Along with Nicodemus, he followed the Jewish burial customs. The watching women who followed must have been so relieved that someone had come forward to perform this important task for their Lord. God sometimes brings people into our lives at just the right moment—perhaps people who are able to help us in specific ways. Share your experiences of this.

- We see in this episode the women wanting to finish anointing the body of Jesus with ointment and spices. We have a need for ritual when someone dies, which is closely linked to our move towards 'closure' (an acknowledgment of the ending of a loved one's life, giving oneself permission to grieve). There is ritual in the funeral or thanksgiving ceremony itself, but also 'ritual' in how we remember someone, such as visiting specific places, looking through photograph albums and so on. There are lesser 'goodbyes' in our lives, where prayer and a certain amount of ritual can enable us to move towards closure. Share examples from your lives.

- Stop and take a moment to pray for people who have never had that closure, whose loved ones are missing, including those who have gone missing in action or are assumed dead although their bodies have never been found. Also pray for the people who support them, such as trauma counsellors.

■ The women were together in their grief. It is important to have a support system, a network of close friends and relatives. Perhaps the group with whom you are exploring these passages provides that network for you. Discuss how such networks have helped you at various stages of life.

■ Mary was let down by her support system: she met with disbelief, and the women would not support her testimony. How do we deal with being let down by those we trusted greatly or when we lose our support system? Share your experiences. How can we recover?

■ David brings this grief to God in Psalm 41:9: 'Even my best friend, the one I trusted completely, the one who shared my food, has turned against me.' After David's honest cries from the heart, in which none of his negative feelings are hidden, he concludes with the faithfulness of God: 'You have brought me into your presence forever. Praise the Lord, the God of Israel, who lives from everlasting to everlasting' (vv. 12–13). We, too, can be uplifted by remembering God's faithfulness.

■ The life of Mary of Magdala illustrates the promise that we can hold on to in all circumstances: 'A bruised reed he will not break, and a smouldering wick he will not snuff out' (Isaiah 42:3, NIV).

■ The risen Christ first appeared to a woman—moreover, to a woman who had been demon-possessed and was then given the momentous task of announcing the resurrection and the future ascension to the disciples. Jesus takes risks with people and trusts where we would not trust. He assigned the church to the care and leadership of Peter, the man who had denied him three times. Our God is the God of the second chance. How does this challenge the way in which we relate to others?

- Mary moved between hope and doubt. Having been told by the angels that Jesus had risen, she told the disciples that she did not know where the Lord's body had been put, but then reported the angels' message that Jesus had risen. We often live with this inner movement between belief and doubt. We, like Mary, may experience God transforming our lives but then, some time later, doubt this change. Our walk with and towards God may seem to spiral rather than moving in a straight line. If you are able, share experiences of your movement between hope and doubt.

- In the New Testament we see Jesus responding with compassion to our genuine struggles between belief and unbelief. We read in Mark 9:23–24 of the conversation between Jesus and a father who wants healing for his son. Jesus said, 'Anything is possible if a person believes' and the father immediately responded, 'I do believe, but help me overcome my unbelief.' Jesus answered the cries of this man and healed his son. We can take comfort from the fact that Jesus singled out Thomas to enable him to overcome his doubts (John 20:24–29).

- Rather than feeling guilty for doubting, it is helpful to remember God's character of love, mercy and faithfulness. You could pray the prayer of David in Psalm 40:11: 'Lord, don't hold back your tender mercies from me. Let your unfailing love and faithfulness always protect me.'

- Mary had an encounter with the risen Christ and returned to the disciples to say, 'I have seen the Lord.' This encounter changed everything for Mary: 'joy replaced despair; light replaced darkness; confidence replaced self-doubt; purpose replaced emptiness'. Your encounter with the risen Christ may have been one of quiet and steady growth in belief or it may have come at a definite moment in time, as did Mary's. Encourage one another with your stories of coming to faith and the difference that it has made in your lives.

- Our belief in Christ's resurrection can be strengthened by studying the intellectual evidence for the resurrection. We are also led into deeper belief and faith by 'receiving' the story of the resurrection through entering the scene in meditation, as we have done through the eyes of Mary of Magdala, and meeting the risen Christ.

- How have you grown in your knowledge of Christ, the Son of God, through these passages?

Conclusion

Take time to pray through your findings. What might God be saying to you? Is anything particularly relevant to your life at the moment? Write down what you have learnt and refer back to it regularly in the days ahead so that it becomes part of your thinking, reacting and lifestyle.

Notes

1   E. Griffin, *Wilderness Time* (HarperOne, 1997) p. 28
2   Westminster Shorter Catechism (1647)
3   Malachi 4:5–6
4   Numbers 6:24–26 (NIV)
5   Luke 1:46–47 (NIV)
6   Luke 1:68–69, 76 (NIV 1984)
7   Psalm 119:1–2, 11, 14–16 (NIV 1984)
8   Luke 1:32–33 (NIV)
9   Luke 1:35 (NIV)
10 Luke 1:38
11 Luke 1:42–45
12 Luke 1:46–55
13 Micah 5:2
14 Luke 2:14
15 Psalm 68:5
16 Psalm 146:9
17 Psalm 147:3
18 Isaiah 54:5
19 Isaiah 54:6
20 Malachi 4:2
21 Luke 2:29–32 (NIV 1984)
22 Luke 2:34–35 (NIV)
23 Isaiah 40:1–2
24 Isaiah 9:6 (NIV)
25 Matthew 2:6; see Micah 5:2
26 'O worship the Lord in the beauty of holiness' by John Monsell (1863)
27 Mark 5:35–43
28 Mark 9:1–10
29 John 11:21–22
30 John 11:25–26
31 John 12:7–8

32 Gary Chapman has written a helpful book called *The Five Love Languages*. Visit www.5lovelanguages.com to discover more about this concept and find out what your love language is.

33 Mark 15:34 (NIV)

34 Matthew 12:49–50

35 Luke 4:18–19; the prophecy is from Isaiah 61:1–2

36 Luke 4:21

37 Matthew 13:55–56

38 Luke 4:23–24

39 Luke 4:25–27

40 Psalm 5:2 (NIV 1984)

41 Matthew 13:57

42 Mark 3:20–21

43 John 7:4 (NIV)

Meditating with Scripture: John's Gospel

Using the ancient tradition of lectio divina

Elena Bosetti

'*How should we read the Gospel of John? There are so many ways. The one presented here is rooted in an experience that does not separate reason from faith or the intellect from the heart. It follows the method of* lectio divina, *proposes a prayerful listening to the word and is moved by the invocation of the Spirit. We cannot fly on eagle's wings unless the Spirit lifts us.*'

Using the ancient tradition of *lectio divina* ('sacred reading'), this book leads us through John's Gospel, reflecting on the people and events in the life of Jesus, as well as his teaching and prayers, which combine to make this most carefully structured and lyrical of Gospel accounts. Each chapter ends with exercises to help us 'dialogue with the word' and a prayerful meditation to help shape our response.

ISBN 978 1 84101 823 2   £7.99
Available from your local Christian bookshop or, in case of difficulty, direct from BRF: please visit www.brfonline.org.uk.

Discovering the Spiritual Exercises of Saint Ignatius

Larry Warner

This book is an adaptation of the Spiritual Exercises of St Ignatius Loyola, to help you to embark on a life-transforming journey toward Christlikeness. For nearly 500 years, the Exercises have been a tool for spiritual formation. During those years their popularity has ebbed and flowed, but they are now experiencing something of a revival across the breadth of the Church.

This is not a book about the methods or techniques of Christian formation but one that enables you to come before God through the Gospel narratives in order to encounter Jesus afresh. If you hunger for something deeper, yearn to walk with Jesus (not just read about him) and desire to embrace more of what God is doing in and through you, then this is the book for you.

ISBN 978 1 84101 883 6   £10.99
Available from your local Christian bookshop or direct from BRF: visit www.brfonline.org.uk

Embracing Dusty Detours

A spiritual search for depth in desert places

Lynne E. Chandler

'I feel at last that I am embracing the present moment of life. I haven't arrived, I'm just resting; resting beside quiet waters that inevitably churn and stir from time to time and turn into strong currents that drag me back into the river of the hectic everyday.'

This book takes you on a quest through the bustling chaos of Middle Eastern city life and the drama of a youth-led revolution to endless stretches of desert sand and Bible places from Mount Sinai to the shores of Galilee. This quest, along life's dusty detours, is in search of oases of all kinds— people, places, and little glimpses of eternity. Lynne's journey involves laughter, tears and raw honesty, and is often one lurch forward and two steps backward, but it has led her to deeper insights into faith and greater reliance on God than she ever imagined.

ISBN 978 1 84101 829 4   £6.99

Available from your local Christian bookshop or direct from BRF: visit www.brfonline.org.uk

Time for Reflection

Meditations to use through the year

Ann Persson

It is not easy to switch from activity to stillness, from noise to silence, from achieving to letting go, from doing to being in the presence of God. This book of biblically rooted meditations provides accessible and practical routes to exploring prayer as that way of being in God's presence, letting the sediment of our lives settle so that we may have a true reflection of ourselves and of God within us.

Loosely based around the seasons of the Church year and also drawing inspiration from the seasons of nature, the meditations range from short 'spaces for grace' to longer exercises that can form the basis for a personal quiet day or retreat.

ISBN 978 1 84101 876 8   £8.99
Available from your local Christian bookshop or direct from BRF:
visit www.brfonline.org.uk

(Extra)Ordinary Women

Reflections for women on Bible-based living

Clare Blake

Have you ever felt that women in the Bible were superstars, somehow extra specially blessed by God? And then looked at yourself...?

This book of down-to-earth Bible reflections is based around the central theme that all women are special in God's eyes. Relating scriptural teaching to everyday experience, it shows how God has a special gifting for each of us, how we can turn to him when life doesn't make sense, and how to set about discovering his will for our lives.

Taking a fresh look at the stories of Sarah, Leah, Mary, and other Bible characters, we see how God looks beyond our failures and weaknesses to the women he has created us to be aas we learn to follow him, step by step.

ISBN 978 1 84101 235 1   £6.99
Available from your local Christian bookshop or direct from BRF: visit www.brfonline.org.uk

Enjoyed
this book?

Write a review—we'd love to hear what you think.
Email: reviews@brf.org.uk

Keep up to date—receive details of our new books as they happen.
Sign up for email news and select your interest groups at:
www.brfonline.org.uk/findoutmore/

Follow us on Twitter @brfonline

By post—to receive new title information by post (UK only), complete the form below and post to: BRF Mailing Lists, 15 The Chambers, Vineyard, Abingdon, Oxfordshire, OX14 3FE

Your Details
Name _____
Address_____
_____
Town/City _____ Post Code _____
Email_____

Your Interest Groups (*Please tick as appropriate)	
☐ Advent/Lent	☐ Messy Church
☐ Bible Reading & Study	☐ Pastoral
☐ Children's Books	☐ Prayer & Spirituality
☐ Discipleship	☐ Resources for Children's Church
☐ Leadership	☐ Resources for Schools

Support your local bookshop
Ask about their new title information schemes.